Zen and the Art of Needlecraft

Exploring the Links Between Needlecraft, Spirituality, and Creativity

Sandra Detrixhe,

Author of *Zen and the Art of Quilting*
The Everything® Quilting Book
The Everything® Sewing Book

ADAMS MEDIA
Avon, Massachusetts

Published by
Adams Media, an F+W Publications Company
57 Littlefield Street, Avon, MA 02322. U.S.A.
www.adamsmedia.com

ISBN: 1-59337-375-9

Printed in Canada.

J I H G F E D C B A

Library of Congress Cataloging-in-Publication Data
Detrixhe, Sandra.
Zen and the art of needlecraft / by Sandra Detrixhe.
p.   cm.
Includes index.
ISBN 1-59337-375-9
1. Sewing--Miscellanea. 2. Needlework--Miscellanea.
3. Zen Buddhism--Influence. I. Title.

TT715.D48 2005
646.2--dc22

2005016017

This publication is designed to provide accurate and authoritative information with
regard to the subject matter covered. It is sold with the understanding that the pub-
lisher is not engaged in rendering legal, accounting, or other professional advice. If
legal advice or other expert assistance is required, the services of a competent professional person should be sought.
—From a *Declaration of Principles* jointly adopted by a Committee of the
American Bar Association and a Committee of Publishers and Associations

Illustrations by Mark Divico

This book is available at quantity discounts for bulk purchases.
For information, please call 1-800-872-5627.

Contents

In memory of my parents,
Leo and Donna Paulsen,
for encouraging me to write
and to sew.

Acknowledgments

I want to thank my editor, Kate Epstein, for all her suggestions, and all the friends who shared their sewing and stitchery stories with me. I've tried to retell your stories as accurately as possible. Please forgive any inadvertent errors. Thank you also to Linda Ashton for the tour of the Scott Specialties factory. And last, a special thanks to my daughter Eden, who acted as first reader for yet another book.

Introduction

Knowing how to sew used to be a necessity. From the time cave dwellers first stitched hides together for clothing or shelter until relatively recent times when factory-produced clothing became widely available, someone in every household needed to know how to sew. In fact, even though much of the sewing fell to women throughout history, until recently most men knew enough sewing to mend harnesses and even replace rent seams and buttons if there were no women around.

Of course, the upper class folk could hire members of the lower class to sew for them. And in their free time wealthy women did handwork: fancy embroidery and cross-stitch. They spent their leisure time enjoying an unnecessary type of sewing.

People who couldn't afford to hire someone to sew made their own clothing and, if they were good at it, found employment sewing for the wealthy. This general arrangement continued from ancient times until the fairly recent past, when garments (and curtains and bedding) began to be mass-produced. For several decades after that, home sewing was still a way of saving a little money. And it was still a necessity for people who were larger or smaller than the standard sizes. Even today it can be difficult for some people to find clothes that fit them well, though not like it was a few decades ago.

Nowadays, economical garments are readily available. Online shopping brings specialty stores to our fingertips. Clothing made offshore by incredibly cheap labor is often less expensive to buy than the same garment would be if we sewed it ourselves. Those of us who still sew do it for reasons that have little to do with necessity or even economics: we love the process. We love the look and feel of cloth: clinging synthetics, durable cottons, shimmering silks. We love the challenge of sewing flat pieces of cloth together to make a three-dimensional garment or craft. We love having (or giving away) something we made with our own hands, something that we transformed from imagination into reality, though perhaps imperfectly. We may even love the hum of our sewing machines and the hot scent of our irons, but I imagine that's because they are sensory experiences of the hobby we love.

Decorative stitching has evolved much the same as construction sewing, becoming an artisan enterprise in a big way during the Middle Ages. The Puritans considered fancywork on clothing a vanity, but the stitchers found expression in pious sayings on samplers. Through the centuries, women have added decorative stitches to clothing and household items to add a personal touch or to increase their value, if only to themselves. Eventually even embroidery work became mass-produced, but some of us still love to stitch.

Any needlecraft, if we do it out of love of the p
decidedly Zen experience. Zen is the Japanese translauv..
Sanskrit word meaning meditation. Zen is a form of Buddhism,
which emphasizes meditation or self-discovery and understanding as a way to enlightenment, rather than studying or following
rules. The goals of Zen practice are threefold. The first is to
balance the mind, or, in other words, to find the right combination of spontaneity and self-control. This is a nice definition of
creativity, don't you think?

The second goal is enlightenment, which is a kind of superalertness. We experience this alertness when we give ourselves
over to our hobbies, leaving the rest of our stressful lives behind
for awhile. We may not discover total, universal understanding,
but often solutions to our own problems come to us once we've
escaped to our stitching.

The third goal is to live that enlightenment in our daily lives.
This one's a little harder. We shift gears so often: from work to
family to hobby to housework to church or other volunteer work
to countless other activities. Half the time, or perhaps more,
we are thinking about everything except the current activity,
the current moment. We look without seeing, hear without listening. We rehearse the future and relive the past, failing to
appreciate the here and now. We need to learn to work and play
mindfully—that is, aware of and appreciating the moment we
are living in. The way to learn to do this is to practice it where
it is easiest to achieve, with our beloved hobby. Sewing with a
measure of Zen awareness just might teach us how to bring that
same peace and joy into the other aspects of our lives.

In my conservative Christian neck of the woods, mention of what I'm writing has raised a few eyebrows. Zen sounds alien and hence frightening. Zen is not a religion, but rather an experience, and is not incompatible with Western religions. You can be a Catholic, Protestant, Jew, atheist, or anything else and practice Zen. The whole point of Zen is to understand our mind—or, put another way, to discover our true nature.

Zen has to do with our inner life, our spirituality, something that too many of us neglect much of the time. But our inner life has a profound effect on our physical health, on our disposition, on our ability to cope with the unexpected difficulties that life all too often throws at us. From a Zen perspective, hobbies such as sewing enrich our lives well beyond the obvious products of our efforts. They heal us emotionally—like meditation, which is the essence of Zen.

chapter one

Adventures in Needlecraft

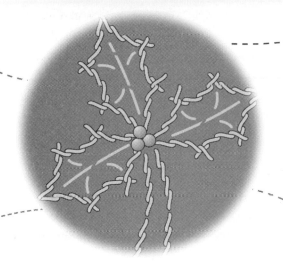

Tip: Get Organized

It's a good idea to regularly organize and clean the area where you craft and/or store materials. Each handwork project should have an appropriate basket or bag to keep all the materials together and to keep them clean. In the sewing room, dust picked up and carried on your thread will clog the tension discs and bobbin area of your sewing machine. Clutter will increase your chances of losing pieces of your project. A reasonably orderly space will attract you and free your creativity. If your supplies must be packed away, organize your storage for easiest access. Label the pieces of your project before you store them away to save time when you get them out again.

Raiding Mom's Stash

I remember making doll clothes by hand long before I was allowed to use the sewing machine. A particular little gathered skirt stands out in my memory. I was probably about seven.

I cut a rectangle out of fabric from my mother's box of scraps. I ran a row of hand stitches in and out along one long side of my rectangle, pulled the thread up to make gathers, and tied the thread in a knot. I was careful to check this against the waist of my doll before I tied it off, something I must have learned from past mistakes. I was so proud of myself! Clearly I had invented gathers, or, at the very least, discovered on my own the best way to make them.

Next, I cut a strip of cloth about ½" wide without the aid of any kind of measuring device or straightedge. This strip was long enough to go around my doll's waist and overlap a little. I was glad that I had thought of the need for the ends to overlap. I sewed this strip over the top of my gathers. At the skirt bottom, I overlapped an inch or so and stitched that down with the same in-and-out running stitch and huge external knots.

Last, I sewed a snap to the ends of the waistband. This was always difficult because the snaps were tiny, and I wanted to use the smallest I could find in my mother's sewing supplies. If I wasn't careful, I might sew one half on upside down and then the snap wouldn't work. When that happened, I had to try to cut the threads without cutting the fabric. There were always a lot of threads to cut since I took about a dozen stitches in each hole with my doubled-over thread. My dolls' snaps and buttons never fell off like my shirt buttons did sometimes.

Besides the difficulty of manipulating tiny snaps into place, my little fingers couldn't sew with a single strand of thread without having it constantly slipping off the needle. Mom taught me to double the thread over and tie both ends together in a knot. This worked great until I made a mistake. With single thread you simply slide off the needle and pull out the wrong stitch. When the thread is doubled, you have to cut the thread and start over. I remember trying to poke the needle back through the cloth in exactly the spot where it came out to undo a misplaced stitch. Sometimes it actually worked.

However, on this particular day, none of these potential pitfalls prevented me from making a skirt for my doll. I remember thinking that the skirt showed that I was now an expert seamstress. After all, I had had two, maybe three years' experience.

My sister Nora, who is a year and twelve days my senior, remembers Mom teaching us to thread a needle when we were very young—even before Nora started to school. There was no kindergarten in the country school we would attend, so the sewing lessons had to have taken place sometime before her sixth and my fifth birthdays. It's quite possible that at the time that I made my wonderful skirt, I was using Mom's sharp sewing scissors to cut out doll clothes and doll pillows at home but was required to use round-tipped scissors at school.

At about the same time, we began experimenting with embroidery. I remember Mom taking tea towels out of the drawer and ironing transfers onto them for us to stitch. I know that I tied my ends in knots instead of burying the tails. Tying the knots and threading the needle were difficult for me, so I tried to sew with ridiculous lengths of thread. These tangled hopelessly, of course. I also remember using all six strands of embroidery floss. If anyone was giving me instructions, I wasn't paying much attention. I was a little short on patience for that kind of work anyway. I wanted to move on to what I imagined would be more exciting adventures in needlecraft.

From the time Nora and I mastered the rudiments of hand stitching, we began begging to use the sewing machine. Mom's response was always, "When you're twelve." Nora remembers this as Mom's standard response to all unreasonable requests, but I only remember it in relation to the sewing machine. Nora says that on her twelfth birthday she realized she was already doing all those things she had been told to wait for, making the Big Day a bit of a disappointment. Since I had to do everything as soon as she did, I was using the sewing machine before I turned eleven.

Mom's excuse for putting off the use of the machine was that we would run the needle through a finger, which I did once when I was thirteen or fourteen. I suspect her real reason had more to do with the machine itself. It was an old treadle machine and the tension was easily messed up. She was afraid she wouldn't be able to find replacement needles and didn't want us breaking the few she had.

Before you start imagining that I must have been a little girl in the late 1800s, I'd like to mention that the machine may have been old when Mom got it. I think it had been her mother's. Since electricity wasn't available to most rural Kansas folks like my parents until the 1940s, it would have been the only kind of machine she could have used. After electricity was installed in their home around 1945, Mom didn't like to sew enough to want to replace her mother's sewing machine with an electric one. Consequently, I learned to sew on the treadle machine in the early 1960s.

It had its quirks. You had to start the needle in motion with the hand wheel. If you simply started pedaling, it would run backward, which for some reason would make the thread break. This running-backward business must have been a common problem of the machines. Effie Price, who would have been very close to my mother's age, wasn't allowed to use the sewing machine when she was a girl because her mother was afraid she would tear it up if she ran it backward. Her story is related in Barbara Swell's *Secrets of the Great Old-Timey Cooks* (Asheville, NC: Native Ground Music, Inc., 2001). Effie sewed on the sly when her mother was gone, using her brother as a lookout, and surprised her mother with a finished dress

I suspect that the treadle machine itself was part of the reason Mom didn't like to sew. Besides the fact that she, and we, were always sewing with dull needles, which means that the machine probably skipped stitches, we had to turn the fabric around to backstitch. Forget about zigzag stitches, let alone hem stitches, stretch stitches, or machine embroidery. The machine did only the basic straight stitch and that not too well.

But that old sewing machine made doll-clothes production much more efficient than hand sewing. Nora and I even had Christmas for our dolls one year, making some special present for each one. Even the rattiest hand-me-down doll among them got a home-sewn gift.

These sewing projects were experiments into the nature of cloth and construction, needle and thread. While we wanted the products of our experimentation, the sense of accomplishment must have been more important. Otherwise I wouldn't have such vivid and happy memories of making that particular doll skirt without any recollection of the color or print of the fabric I used to make it.

Mom would help us with specific sewing problems if we brought them to her, usually finding her in the kitchen or the garden. I remember being impressed at some of her solutions! While she gave us full access to her sewing supplies and scraps, she didn't want to actually give us sewing lessons. She was afraid we would feel pressured to sew, which had been her experience as a child.

So Nora and I were left to experiment. The most important thing I learned in those early days was that I love to sew. I can identify with Curlylocks in the old nursery rhyme.

Curlylocks, Curlylocks,
Wilt thou be mine?
Thou shalt not wash dishes
Nor yet feed the swine,
But sit on a cushion
And sew a fine seam,
And feed upon strawberries,
Sugar and cream.

The luxury implied in strawberries and cream is extended to the image of endless time to stitch. What bliss!

My sister Nora, however, learned something equally important. She, like Mom, would find other things she enjoyed more than sewing. Sewing would not become part of her description of the good life. This verse from the 1843 poem "Song of the Shirt" by Thomas Hood, though a bit extreme, might better reflect her image of sewing:

> With fingers weary and worn,
> With eyelids heavy and red,
> A woman sat in unwomanly rags
> Plying her needle and thread—
> Stitch! Stitch! Stitch!
> In poverty, hunger, and dirt.

Beginner's Mind

These two poems illustrate the two prevailing images of needlecraft. The difference, I suppose, is similar to the difference between necessary sewing (drudgery) and unnecessary sewing (fun). There seems to be a line here between fancywork and construction sewing, though very little construction sewing is necessary these days.

But people do seem to either hate to sew (cross-stitch, embroider, whatever) or they love it. The only neutral folks would be those who have never tried it. Even among them there is likely to be a comment such as "I wish I had time" ("knew how," "had the resources," etc.) or an emphatic "I don't sew."

Among those of us who tried some form of needlecraft, whether at age four or sixty-four, and fell in love with it, there is usually a desire to learn more, try something different, stretch ourselves in some way. The doing is more important than the project itself. This is a fundamental aim of Zen: to experience life completely, to understand yourself, your whole mind, and your place in the world.

So much of our lives is routine. We neither look nor listen nor feel this particular moment, let alone appreciate it. We are always projecting ahead or remembering back. This moment is lost even as we live it.

However, when we lose ourselves in a favorite hobby we are more aware of the here and now. We are watching our stitches closely, attuned to the sound of our sewing machines, aware of every inch of springy yarn as we feed it to our knitting needles or mentally measuring or even counting each tiny cross-stitch.

This may be especially true when we are beginners. We feel a need to watch so many things at once. At seventeen, Nora's youngest child, Daniel, remembers being very nervous about sewing when he was learning some ten years ago. He compares it to bungee jumping, or at least what he imagines bungee jumping would be like. There was all the tension built up from all the instructions from Mom and helpful older sisters. "Don't poke your finger" seemed like a dire warning when it had been repeated several times. But Danny took the plunge and when the cord sprang he had a peaceful thought: "It's only sewing."

Zen masters talk about Beginner's Mind. This is the ability to experience everything as if for the first time. If we let them, fears, prejudices, opinions, and the whole realm of our past experiences will color how we see each moment and keep us from experiencing the here and now as it truly is. To achieve Beginner's Mind, we need to put all these things aside, let them go. When we do, there are all sorts of possibilities.

Projects designed specifically to teach us a new skill help us experience Beginner's Mind. This is true whether we are experimenting or taking lessons from someone else. After a few years of playing at sewing, I knew there was a limit to what I was going to learn by experimenting alone. In a sense I was reinventing the wheel with every effort. To learn how to "really sew," I turned to 4-H. The whole 4-H program is rather Zen itself with "Learning by Doing" as its motto. Nora and I joined the club when we were nine and eight, respectively.

Mom had some resistance to my enrolling in the sewing project. Her argument was that she wouldn't be able to help me with my sewing. I figured that that was part of the point of 4-H: some other mom could teach me how to do the things mine couldn't teach me. This argument didn't work as well as I thought it would. I realized later that implicit in that logic was the notion that my mom would return the favor by being a leader in some other project that included other 4-H members. She didn't want to do that.

Dad, however, was willing to lead a project once in a while and finally, when I was thirteen, I was allowed to enroll in "Let's Sew, It's Fun." Mariesther Holbert was the instructor and there were a couple of other girls along with Mariesther's two daughters and me. I remember having little interest in the actual items

I needed to sew to fulfill the requirements of the project, but I was very pleased to be doing them. Mom even arranged for me to borrow a sewing machine from another of my sisters, Nancy, who was married and had a portable machine. I had electric power in my stitching now!

At the time, I had no idea how common that excitement was. Years later, Nancy's grandson, Kyler, wanted to learn to sew because his mother's machine looked like such fun. He enrolled in the sewing project in 4-H when he was twelve and made pajamas and a bathrobe. It proved more difficult to stitch a straight seam than he had expected, and his mom made him redo the collar several times. He turned out to be one of those rare males who is willing to follow directions, however.

My nephew Danny remembers that he fantasized that he was driving a car when he first began using a sewing machine. That thought probably crossed my mind and the minds of other predriving sewers. We called the foot pedal the gas pedal and would say "put her in reverse" to backstitch and things like that. But the idea was usually fleeting, as the need to keep the fabric moving correctly under the needle took our full concentration.

Mariesther taught me how to lay out a pattern, and I made my first dress under her tutelage. I actually liked the dress, but the other things I made don't even sound familiar when I look back through my old 4-H records. But I remember the sewing sessions at the Holbert home and Nancy's sewing machine on a card table in the dining room.

4-H also offered a knitting project, which I enrolled in and enjoyed, earning a few nice awards before I was through, but fancywork needlecrafts such as cross-stitch and embroidery hadn't really found a place in the program, yet. I think most of my friends thought that kind of activity was only for old ladies, so I happily stitched away in private.

When I was in junior high and high school, Home Economics was required for the girls and included part of a semester of sewing. I noticed quickly that there were more rules and fewer shortcuts taught in the Home Economics classes than there had been in 4-H. The nature of 4-H, with its volunteer instructors, is probably the reason. Repinning an entire pattern layout to the fabric so that all the pins run in the same direction to make it more "convenient" later was not something Mariesther would have made us do. The rules, however, are always good to know. It's best to be aware of what rules you are breaking. Sometimes, your favorite shortcut might not work with a particular pattern or fabric, and you'll need to fall back on the rules for help.

In a sense, at those times when you are faced with a new kind of fabric or a new technique, Beginner's Mind can actually come to your rescue. For example, if you are dealing with a wool plaid, what you learned working with cotton prints isn't going to be much help. You need to look at the wool plaid as if you are just learning to sew. And if you know how to cross-stitch, regular embroidery can seem like a whole new art to learn.

Beginner's Mind doesn't mean not learning from your experiences. Everything that happens to you becomes part of you. You can't really leave them all behind, but you need to keep from letting them limit you. It means that you open yourself up to this moment and experience it with your whole mind, with the kind of absorbed interest of a beginner. Enlightenment is sometimes described as reality unhampered by ideas.

Perhaps this is easier for children. They haven't accumulated so many prejudices as adults. I think it's these prejudices that keep us from trying something new, prejudices like those expressed in the two poems I cited earlier: "Only poor people need to sew," or "Only rich people have time to sew." We can also be stopped in our tracks by thoughts like "I'll never be able to cross-stitch as well as Mom (my sister, my friend, or whoever) so I won't even try." "Satins (wools, corduroy, metallic thread) are too hard to work with." "I can't follow a pattern," or "I can't make . . . " (fill in the blank with whatever gives you pause).

Here's the wonder of Beginner's Mind. None of those things matter. There's only the here and now, this pattern or idea, this piece of cloth. This chance to be creative. This chance to try something new.

Pass It On

The truth is, nowadays we don't absolutely need to know how to make clothes. This wasn't always true. My husband's grandmother, Minnie Benson, was just a child when her mother died in 1900. Her father knew it was important that Minnie learn how to cook, clean house, and sew. The first two, he or his older daughters could teach her, but he worried about the last one. He sent her to live with a neighbor woman for a time, a summer perhaps, so she would learn to sew. She went on to raise three girls, sewed all their clothes while they were growing up, and continued to sew all her life. When she was around eighty she made aprons for her daughters and her grandsons' wives for Christmas, which, I'm happy to say, included me.

My mother when she was a girl hated having to stay indoors and learn to sew, embroider, and crochet while her older brothers were off on seemingly wonderful adventures. Her mother, however, was trying to teach her something that was necessary at the time. Mom was born in 1913, and while ready-made clothing was available, a good homemaker was expected to make most of the family's clothes as well as curtains and other household decorations.

If Mom ever made anything for me, it was when I was very young. I know, because of her large stash of fabric, that she had sewn in earlier years, when her first four children, her "first family" so to speak, were young. By the time Nora and I came along, trailers that we were, she felt prosperous enough to buy all our clothes. She talked sometimes about her sewing experiences, usually in less than glowing terms.

She was a young farm wife during the Depression, when cash became frighteningly scarce. She would try to save feed sacks to sew with, as many women did. Companies that made feed for chickens used cotton prints for their bags to attract women, who were often the ones with the responsibility of caring for the family flock.

The practice continued into the late 1940s or early 1950s. My husband remembers going to the feed store with his mother when he was a small boy. He thought the store was beautiful with all the stacks of colorful bags for his mother to choose from. By then, the Depression was over and his family was doing fairly well financially. Lucille was able to buy some feed ahead based on how much fabric she wanted.

My mother's recollection was of trying to save enough sacks to make herself a dress only to have a fabric print discontinued before she had enough. Her situation was not such that she could afford to buy much ahead.

I remember trying to picture feed sacks, which I thought were like the burlap my dad used to sack up the alfalfa seed he raised. Since I didn't know about patterns and shaping, I pictured my mother wearing a burlap bag and thought she was lucky they ran out before she got enough. I know now that they were pretty cotton prints and probably my mother's best chance at a new dress. The feed-sack experience may have been the final discouragement for my mother. I don't remember seeing her use the machine for anything but mending.

For me sewing was simply play, like cutting out paper dolls or stacking building blocks. My experience of beginning to sew with doll clothes isn't uncommon, but it isn't universal, either. My daughter didn't make doll clothes, that I know of, because she had very little interest in dolls. While there is something to be said for experimenting, there's also nothing wrong with seeking help when you decide to learn, however old you are.

For some of the women I talked to, the fact that their mothers sewed made it seem like something they should do. My friend Nancy Collins said that her mother did all the sewing for her and her sisters. The machine was always set up in one corner or another. Nancy in turn did all the sewing for her two children and still makes nearly all of her own clothes.

On the other hand, I have talked to women who said the reason they don't sew is because their mothers did so much of it. It was easier and faster for their mothers to make something for them than it would have been for her to teach them how to do it for themselves. Some of those women have come to sewing later, usually to their mothers' delight.

Few of my friends learned their stitchery skills from their mothers. Perhaps their mothers were too busy for these more time-consuming projects. Also, cross-stitch and embroidery, while they are very popular now, were considered old-fashioned when I and my friends were young. Our grandmothers probably did more handwork than our mothers because fancy needle-work fit with the decorating ideas of their time. By the 1950s and '60s when I was young, "clean" was in: clean lines, easily laundered, unadorned was the ideal.

I think the fact that my mother didn't like to sew is the reason she let me have full access to her sewing supplies. I'm not sure I would have been able to turn everything over to my daughter the same way. Like my mother, I didn't want to push my daughter to sew. I was well aware by the time Eden was three or four that she didn't necessarily like what I liked at her age. She showed little interest in sewing, at least it seemed to me, until she discovered cross-stitch. That became her craft of choice, and she surpassed my skill very quickly.

Eden's interest in construction sewing developed more recently. She served as first reader for me while I wrote *The*

Everything® Quilting Book. She started with a queen-sized quilt, not your usual first sewing project, then branched out to pajama bottoms and other things as she previewed, critiqued, and edited two other sewing books for me. I guess I did finally teach her to sew even if it was via e-mailed chapters.

My sister Nora, who doesn't really like to sew, actually did a better job of passing the skill on to her children. She felt that teaching her children to sew was part of being a good mother. She taught each of her five children, boys included, because she believed that they needed to be able to sew on a button, at the very least. Her conviction was reinforced by her local school district: it required that all students take Home Economics, which included a unit of sewing.

She's not as successful as she had hoped, even with the school's help. Her older son, Kevin, now in his twenties, will beg his sisters to sew on buttons for him when he's home.

The girls showed some interest, though. Nora's youngest daughter, Kimberly, did me one better in her childhood doll skirt: elastic. And Nora's middle child, Amy, is the one most likely to continue sewing all her life.

I think Nora feels a little guilty that the others don't sew, thinking she should have taught them better or set a better example. I doubt if there was much she could have done, or even should have done. Eunice Farmer, who writes the syndicated newspaper column "Sew Simple," mentioned recently in her column that only one of her three daughters likes to sew.

Nothing you do for a child is ever wasted, they say. You just don't always know what the child will do with it later. Michael

DeBakey's mother taught him to sew when he was five. Raheeja DeBakey was such an accomplished seamstress, a few neighbors asked her to teach their daughters. Michael hung around during the classes out of curiosity, but with his mother's encouragement, soon joined in.

Since he wasn't in school yet, he had the benefit of much more instruction than the regular students. His mother's beautiful work was inspiring and her instruction kind and gentle. In the 1950s, Michael, now a surgeon, developed a graft for replacing a diseased aorta. He drew the design on paper the way his mother had taught him fifty years before. He cut the pattern out of Dacron, a synthetic cloth that was new at the time, and sewed the prototype together on his wife's sewing machine. In an article he wrote for *Time* magazine in August, 2004, he credits his mother's compassion and generosity for his life spent trying to make people feel better, and her sewing lessons for his ability to design the lifesaving graft.

Sometimes mothers and daughters (or sons) don't have the best teacher/student relationships. Karla McMillan, a friend and fellow farm wife, does a lot of sewing now, but didn't learn much from her mother. As a 4-H leader, her mother taught others to sew but didn't have any patience with her own children. Karla learned more at school and from her grandmother, and later from her mother-in-law. In fact it's been her mother-in-law she's called on if she had a problem with a pattern.

When it came time to teach her daughter to sew, she was very conscious of the need for patience. If she felt herself becoming frustrated, she would try to take a break. Her daughter,

Ashley, claims it was a horrible ordeal but didn't do too badly with her 4-H sewing. She won grand champion one year and reserve champion another. She shocked her mother recently during a trip home from college when she said she might like to have a sewing machine.

Mariesther, my 4-H sewing leader, would agree that it doesn't always work to teach your own children to sew. Karen, her older daughter, was interested and therefore easy to teach. She still sews. Deanna, however, had no interest and hated being forced to learn. Mariesther felt that Deanna disrupted class with her attitude. I think I remember just a little of that tension at the sewing meetings. Of course, my main concern was getting my own sewing figured out, so it didn't bother me much. I'm sure Mariesther felt the stress of having an unhappy child (armed with pins and scissors) while she was trying to teach the class.

Mariesther's own mother had taught her and it had been a good experience. But then, Mariesther had wanted to learn. That's probably a much bigger factor than the instructor in most cases. Sometimes a child simply picks up sewing without anyone making a real effort to teach her. My neighbor Jane Snavely remembers sewing before she started school. Her mother sewed and so did her grandmother. She remembers sitting under her grandmother's quilt frame and pushing the needle back through the quilt as a way of "helping" her grandmother. I'd imagine Grandma had to take out all of those stitches after Jane left, but it was a game that made sewing seem fun to Jane.

Jane also had an aunt who pieced quilt tops that a partner quilted. They sold the quilts all over the country. This attitude toward sewing left an impression as well. Now Jane makes custom curtains and sells original stuffed animals and pillows at craft shows and gift shops. And, like her aunt, she takes hand sewing with her nearly everywhere she goes.

When we are teaching needlecraft to our children, we need to be careful that our lessons are age appropriate. One Christmas when I was probably five, Nora and I each received a little sewing basket, an embroidery hoop, and some embroidery floss. My first effort created a huge tangle of thread. I remember throwing it down and running off to my room saying, "I'm just too little." This didn't earn me the sympathy I was hoping for. My mom and teen-age sister simply turned their attention to Nora.

It's funny to look back on that incident now when I have several needlecraft projects going all the time, materials collected for several more, and wonderful plans almost constantly forming in my head. For one brief moment, I was ready to give up. Even then, I left a door open. I was too little, but I would grow. Even in my frustration, I wanted to stitch.

Whether we make doll clothes, a full-sized quilt, or a little embroidered picture on a tea towel, our learn-to-sew projects teach us more than simply how to sew. They teach us about our particular likes and dislikes, our talents, our level of patience, and much more. They help us know ourselves, which

 Try This

Stretch yourself. Try making something new. Consider it a learning project and don't worry too much about its finished quality. If you've never sewn before, hem up a tablecloth or make a tote bag. If you're an experienced sewer, try something new, such as pants or a quilt. If you love handwork, try your hand at Hardanger lace or stumpwork. Notice how your Beginner's Mind makes you concentrate on the details. Then try bringing that kind of alertness to something routine.

chapter two

New Threads

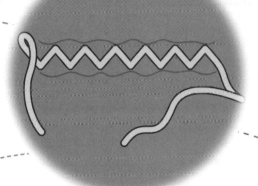

Tip: Threads

When you are machine-sewing, polyester thread will shed less lint than cotton-wrapped polyester (dual duty) and is sometimes recommended by sewing machine manufacturers. It is more expensive but may be worth it if you find your tension repeatedly clogged with lint. If it's available, use mercerized cotton thread for hand sewing. It will tangle less than polyester or dual duty thread. If your thread wants to tangle, try rubbing a sheet of fabric softener over the length of it or try sewing with shorter lengths of thread. Embroidery thread should be cut to the desired length then separated into individual strands. Recombine the threads in twos or threes depending on your project. Your work will be smoother if the strands are not twisted together. Crewel yarn needs to be cut 18" or shorter or it'll break before you're finished.

Identity Outfits

After that first dress I made in 4-H, I made a lot more clothes for myself. I can remember my dad making a comment about my knitting and sewing getting me some "different" outfits. I think that was a nice way of saying that I made a lot of weird clothes, which was true. I think I realized it even then. I made things more because I wanted to make them than because I wanted to have them. Or, perhaps, by the time they were done, they weren't as cool as I thought they'd be. I couldn't admit that, of course, so I had to wear them. About a third of my wardrobe was hand-me-downs from a sister ten years older than me. One would think I would have been more practical, wanting to replace those out-of-style clothes with some more-timely staples. But, no, I made weird stuff.

I remember a dress I made when I was in high school that was two shades of solid blue permanent press cotton/polyester. I made the gathered skirt light blue and the bodice a combination of dark and light blue to look like a vest. Sort of. I embroidered some light blue flowers on the "vest" and similar dark blue ones around the bottom of the skirt, of my own design, of course. (It actually sounds better than it looked.) I had pictured something sort of Swiss and found the pattern that came closest to what I wanted.

As if the appearance wasn't memorable enough, it was my first experience with a hidden zipper. They were a new innovation that, except for the little teardrop-shaped pull hanging at the top, looked nearly like a seam. Of course the plastic zipper teeth were stiffer than the fabric so they didn't bend quite like a seam. The early ones at least also had a tendency to open in the center. They were self-healing, meaning that if you unzipped them and zipped them back up, they'd close again. It was hard for me to trust them, though, after the one in that particular dress opened up in the middle of a choir performance. The "Swiss" dress became my first experience with replacing a zipper.

This dress and others I made were experiments, not only in sewing techniques but also in who I was—or, more accurately, who I wanted to be at the moment.

The clothes we wear are what the world first sees of us and are an outward sign of who we are. As a teenager, I didn't really know who I was. I was trying out personalities along with the different (and I mean *different*, even for the 1960s) clothes. Most of the time young people make the opposite choice— wanting clothes that look just like their friends' clothes—and I did that, too, with store-bought clothes. Sewing and knitting were creative expressions and I didn't want to waste them copying somebody else.

Appearance can be deceiving, of course. We are conscious when we shop or sew for ourselves that we want the clothes to make us look good. Usually this means choosing a color that compliments our complexion and hair color and a style that minimizes the part(s) of our shape that we think are less than perfect.

There's a factor at work on the flip side of this that we may not be aware of. The clothes, and even the colors, we choose affect our mood, or at the very least reflect it. For example, if we are feeling inferior we might choose to wear subdued colors— shades of brown or gray, perhaps. We might choose simple, even unflattering, styles. Unfortunately, wearing these outfits can make us feel even more inferior.

In fact, scientists have found that colors cause physiological changes in our brains. Colors can depress, energize, calm, make us feel cooler or warmer, even increase our appetite. They call this chromodynamics, but really, we've known about it forever. Expressions such as "seeing red" or "feeling blue" come from this ancient knowledge.

For example, bright red is an intense color and actually stimulates a faster heartbeat. Wearing red might pep you up if you're feeling down, but it might also make you look heavier. If you're not an outgoing person, or not feeling outgoing at the moment, you will probably feel very self-conscious calling that much attention to yourself. If you're trying to come out of your shell, however, adding a little bright red trim to the next dress you make might be worth a try. See how it makes you feel. I have a couple of bright red dresses in my closet. Sometimes I'm hesitant to wear either; other times I feel an almost defiant need to wear one.

On the other hand, red is my favorite color to cross-stitch or embroider with. I can't wait to get to the red part but get tired of blue very quickly. Blue causes the body to produce calming chemicals. If you are an emergency room attendant, you ought to wear blue. If you are depressed, you might be attracted to blue fabric, which could make you more depressed. Moving directly to the reds will probably seem too jarring, so head for the more soothing greens or the cheerful yellows.

Color Power

While we can use our color choices to encourage ourselves out of some emotional extremes, the real benefit of knowing how colors affect us is more an exercise in self-discovery. Most of us can name our favorite color, but sometimes we fool ourselves. Check your closet. Is one color or group of colors dominant? Do you know why? Is it truly your favorite color or one you've been told is flattering?

My closet has a lot of blue because I've been told since I was small that it brings out the blue in my eyes. This makes more sense to me now than it did when I was little and wondered how that let my brown-eyed sister wear all the pink. Now my closet has a lot of pink in it, too, because I like it. Next to earth tones, pink is my favorite color to knit or crochet with.

Colors have symbolic meanings as well as physiological ones. Often they are so deeply held we aren't consciously aware of them. Most of these are cultural rather than universal. For instance, in the United States black denotes authority and power. It's also the color of mourning, and too much black can seem evil. White symbolizes innocence and purity and is the color of weddings. In China, white is the funeral color and red is the wedding color.

Black is still accepted as a funeral color in the United States, but in the 1800s, a widow was expected to wear black for a period of mourning that lasted one year and one day and it was scandalous if she didn't. Black was also a fashion color at the time, so it couldn't immediately be assumed that every woman wearing black was in mourning. If a widow didn't own a black dress, she would often dye something black. Her phases of grief might be reflected in the gradual fading of the black dye from the garment. It was up to her to decide when she traded her black garb for purple or gray, then finally resumed wearing other colors again. Or she might add white cuffs and collar to a black outfit to signal that she was in a later stage of mourning.

The purpose of mourning clothes was to alert others that she had lost a loved one and wouldn't be interested in small talk. Men often wore black armbands for the same reason, though they weren't expected to do so for as long. Presumably they had to get on with the business of making a living.

People in mourning were not expected to attend social gatherings, since they would cast a pall on the event. When a woman changed to purple garments or added light-colored trim, she was signaling her desire to socialize again.

The extent to which women followed the prescribed rituals depended on economics; not everyone could afford to replace her wardrobe with black. Also, her age was a factor. A very young widow could be forgiven for cutting her mourning short if she had a child who needed a father, while a woman past middle age might wear black for the rest of her life.

Scarlett O'Hara in Margaret Mitchell's *Gone with the Wind*

hates wearing black when she is widowed young. She follows the social expectations, not to inform others of her mourning—the actual purpose of the custom—but because she is afraid of what others will think of her if she doesn't. They might suppose that she didn't love her husband and that she is selfish and vain, which is pretty much the truth. Rhett Butler encourages her to dismiss the custom—he doesn't care what other people think. When Scarlett's year is over, she is delighted to be wearing colors again, resuming her life where she left off. While the book and movie might be the first exposure for many of us to the custom of mourning clothes, when Margaret Mitchell wrote the book in the 1930s, it was still common knowledge, if not followed any longer. This enabled her to use it and Scarlett's reaction to it as a way of revealing her character at that point in the story. The fact that the custom surprises us now shows how these things change.

In a similar way, when we think of baby girls, we probably think of pink blankets and tiny pink and white dresses, but this wasn't always true. In the Middle Ages, blue cloths and ribbons were hung on the cribs of baby boys because it was believed that blue, the color of heaven, would ward off the devil. I'm not sure if they believed that the devil had no interest in little girls or that girls weren't worth protecting, but there was no special color for girls. Much later, while boys were still wrapped in blue blankets even though the original reason was all but forgotten, someone, probably a clothes manufacturer, decided girls needed a color, too, and started the pink-for-girls tradition. We usually consider pink the color of romance, while its darker version, red, is the color of passion.

Blue, besides being tranquil, symbolizes loyalty. Someone might be described as "true blue." In ancient times blue stood for love, which is why brides are supposed to carry something blue along with the old, new, and borrowed items.

Green, because it is the predominant color in nature, symbolizes health. In the Middle Ages it symbolized fertility. It is actually the easiest color on our eyes and therefore refreshing and calming. On the other hand, people who read auras claim that when we're feeling jealous, our auras will contain more green, as in "green with envy." Garments made in some shades of green or yellow can wash out certain complexions. If you think this happens to you, don't give up green entirely. Try different shades of green, especially dark hunter greens.

Yellow is the most difficult color for our eyes to see. Scientists theorize that this is the reason yellow can enhance our concentration. We think of yellow as a cheerful color, and it is most popular for clothing in the spring.

The most recent cultural connotation of yellow is the yellow ribbon. I pinned a small one to my shirt every day when my son Paul and his National Guard unit were deployed to Bosnia. Since Paul knew I would be wearing it daily, he knew I would be thinking of him each time I pinned it on. Also, people knew what the yellow ribbon meant and would ask me whom I had in the service. This whole tradition grew out of a song that was popular more than twenty years ago. Before that, yellow symbolized cowardice or, in more ancient time, death.

Before synthetic dyes were developed, purple was the most expensive dye to make, calling for thousands of purpura snails to make an ounce of dye. Therefore, it became the color of royalty. A very vivid shade of purple is still called royal purple. The painter Leonardo da Vinci and the composer Richard Wagner both believed that purple increased their creativity.

Except among fans of Kansas State University or other schools that use it as one of their school colors, purple is not a common color for clothes. It stands out like red, thus drawing attention to the wearer, and clashes with nearly everything. Jenny Joseph's poem "Warning (When I am an old woman, I shall wear purple)" suggests that wearing purple is inappropriate but can be forgiven of an old lady. The delightful poem has inspired the Red Hat Society, named for another of the inappropriate things that the poet is saving for her old age.

Events, as well as an awareness of advancing years, can make us wish for more self-expression. A shift in the type of clothes we wear can indicate that a shift of another kind has taken place in our lives, perhaps with the startling realization that life is short. As the poem suggests, things like wearing purple shouldn't be put off indefinitely.

Consider again the predominant colors in your closet. What do they tell you about yourself? Are you wearing the colors you really want to wear or the colors you believe you should wear? I think all the blues in my closet are for my practical self, that part of me that writes books about sewing and works for an accountant. Generally they look good on me without particularly standing out. The pinks belong to the part of me that wants to go back to writing romance novels or wants another crack at childhood.

Now take a look at the standouts, those garments that are completely different in color or style than what you normally choose. Do you wear them very often? Chances are the answer is no. If you bought or made them because you loved them, but feel self-conscious wearing them, there may be a side of your personality that you are hesitant to express. Why are you holding back? If you bought the garment at someone else's urging, it may be more appropriate for that person than for you. It may also tell you something about the image you *don't* want to project.

It's possible, of course, that these outfits hang unworn because they are only appropriate for specific occasions. This will probably be due more to their style than to their color. If you regret not getting to wear a particular garment more, ask yourself if it's because of the garment itself or the type of occasions it's appropriate for. Are these the types of events that you could, or would want to, seek out? For example, you can't wear that dancing dress unless you go dancing.

As you go through your closet it's all right to do some house-cleaning. Clothes that are just taking up space should be passed on to charity. But don't be judgmental, berating yourself for earlier choices. You've changed and so have fashions. This is an exercise in self-discovery, and as such, it should be fun. If it affects your choices in the future, that's fine, too. Zen is more interested in now and where you go from here than in the past. Ask yourself if there's a new you that you want to develop and sew for.

While you're cleaning out your closet you might discover clothes that don't fit. Many of us have weight issues. I know I'm not the only one who has three sizes of clothes crowding up the closet. Some diet experts say we should get rid of any too-large garments when we lose weight. The theory is that if you start to regain the weight, clothes that are getting snug will help motivate you to lose the weight again. If you can simply pull out something larger, you'll ignore the problem until a few pounds become many pounds.

Also, keeping your fat clothes is admitting that you don't really believe you'll keep the weight off. You need to be confident that you've actually changed your lifestyle or you're admitting defeat already.

I get rid of my too-large clothes and get more serious about eating right and exercising whenever things start to feel tight. What I have trouble parting with are the favorites a size or two too small that go back years and years. Most of them, if I ever get into them again, will go straight to the thrift shop. But I want to get into them first. They're my incentive.

Of course, if you're a young woman who may get pregnant some day, you're going to change sizes several times, before and after the baby. You'll probably want to save your favorites from among even the largest sizes. But keep in mind that a few new clothes can help fight the blues if they happen to hit.

Dressing Your True Self

Zen teaches us that the universe is a single interdependent whole. There is no separation between ourselves and the things around us. The molecules that make up your skin touch the molecules of your clothes, which touch the molecules of the air, and so on. Any separation (or suggested superiority) between us and the objects and persons in the room (or world) with us are merely imagined.

This isn't a concept that the Western mind will easily grasp. Beyond the concept that we are all equal in the eyes of God, I'm not sure that it's particularly helpful. Until, that is, we consider what we wear. Since childhood we have probably judged others by what they wear without even realizing it, though sometimes we are aware when others are doing the same to us. From uniforms to culturally significant dress, what we wear gives others a hint about what we do, where we come from, and sometimes our religion and our social status. What we wear is so much a part of who we are that it bears some consideration. Analyzing what we choose to buy or sew for ourselves can tell us a lot about ourselves, but understanding ourselves better might also change how we dress. Your true self or essence is described by Zen masters as your original face, "the face you had before your parents were born."

The more we become distinctly our true selves, the more we see our place in the universe. Our increased spirituality might lead us to decide we won't wear fur, for example. Or perhaps we might restrict ourselves to domestically raised fur and exclude all wild animal fur. These choices grow out of our sense of self in relation to the world. A word of caution, though. It doesn't necessarily follow that your convictions must be emulated by others. Following what someone else demands you believe or requiring someone to follow you is actually the opposite of Zen.

When we do not understand our own true nature, we are more easily deceived. Take for an example part of the creation story from the book of Genesis in the Bible. Adam and Eve in the garden are blissfully unaware of their true human natures. This makes them vulnerable to the serpent's deception. The forbidden fruit didn't make them like God, as the serpent promised, but rather made them see themselves and their nakedness for the first time. This required them to do some hasty home sewing with fig leaves.

The story is usually interpreted as God punishing Adam and Eve for disobeying and lays all the trials and tribulations of a normal human life at the feet of these two people, or more particularly at Eve's feet, though the serpent usually gets some of the blame.

A Buddhist creation story bears a few similarities. In it, we were all once blissful beings living in joy and on joy. Joy was our sole (and soul) sustenance. I say "our" because, since Buddhists believe in reincarnation, in this story we were all alive in the beginning. One of us—we could call her Eve—ate of the essence of the earth. Seeing how she enjoyed it, the rest of us, like Adam, did likewise. But this made our bodies heavy and earthbound. (There are days when I can relate to that.) In this version, all of our trials and tribulations are blamed on our bodies and the inevitable desires that go with them.

Although it may seem as if our brains hold the essence of who we are, directing all our actions, thoughts, and emotions, we can't really separate our mind from our body. How we feel physically affects our mood while our state of mind affects our physical energy. As we've seen, even how we clothe our body affects our state of mind and vice versa.

A classic story of self-deception is "The Emperor's New Clothes." This is one of Hans Christian Andersen's fairy tales. Andersen was a Dane, like my father's ancestors. Born in 1805, he wrote fairy tales, some original and others based on common folktales of the time. In this familiar tale, the emperor, we are told, cares for nothing but clothes—which, as you can imagine, doesn't make him a very good ruler. It also means that he cares more for his appearance than his true self. His vanity leaves him vulnerable to deception.

Two weavers arrive in town boasting of a wonderful magic cloth that cannot be seen by anyone who is stupid or unfit for his position. The emperor, blind to his own failings, thinks this will be a way to uncover any unfit people among his officials and hires the con men to make him a suit of clothes.

As sometimes happens, the emperor has surrounded himself with yes-men, each of them willing to lie to keep his position. One after another, they are sent to check on the weavers' progress. They all see an empty loom and believe that means they are unfit for their positions. Hoping to save their jobs, they tell the emperor that the fabric is lovely, thus proving to the reader that they are, in fact, unfit. The emperor, when he finally checks on the weavers, is momentarily shocked to learn that he himself is unfit to rule. Having his own interests in mind rather than his country's, he pretends to see the non-existent cloth.

Being thoroughly deluded, the emperor decides to wear his new clothes in a ceremonial procession. The con men help him dress, convincing him that the garments are such a splendid fit that he can't even feel them. The emperor and his close advisors are not alone in their foolishness. The townspeople have heard of the cloth's magic powers and all exclaim over the lovely outfit as the emperor passes. Only a child has enough innocence to declare that the emperor is in his underwear. By this time, of course, the weavers have taken all the gold thread the emperor bought for them along with their wages and fled the kingdom.

Now, none of us are going to be quite this deluded. We wouldn't believe in the magic cloth, though we may not be any more self-aware than the foolish emperor. Some of the outland-ish dresses we occasionally see on celebrities at awards shows remind me of the Emperor's new clothes. Apparently the well-paid designers were able to convince the stars that they looked better in these one-of-a-kind dresses than they actually did. (I'm thinking particularly of the young singer a few years back who looked as if she were wrapped in a swan.)

On a scale closer to our own lives, sales clerks can talk us into purchases we later regret. If they are paid by commission, they are often willing to tell us we look great in something that doesn't really suit our true selves. The clothes we make for ourselves are more likely to be just what we want. We usually make our choices without outside pressure, and we have more to choose from in the way of styles and fabrics.

Dressing Your Spirit

Nearly everything can be looked at in two ways: scientifically and spiritually. We saw this with color: the scientific, biological response to the light waves, and the spiritual response to the cultural symbolism of the colors. This is true with styles, too. There is the optical illusion created by the lines of a jacket, for example, that can make you look thinner or taller. Then there is the spiritual lift you can get from wearing a style that presents your true self.

This is why decorated sweatshirts, vests, and denim shirts are popular for casual wear. We can stitch or appliqué anything that suits us and then essentially wear an announcement of our favorite hobby or holiday, or simply things we like.

My friend Nancy Collins, who makes virtually all of her clothes, has collected a set of patterns that reflect what she likes to wear as well as what she likes to sew. Most of them are patterns that allow for some variations so she can use them again and again without seeming to. She says that sometimes she thinks she should quit using a pattern she's used so many times because it's probably becoming obvious that all her jackets, say, are cut alike. But once a pattern is altered to fit just right, she hates to let it go.

An inventory of my patterns reveals something quite different. Each of my dress patterns, for example, was bought for a specific style that I wanted to try. Oh, I could vary the length and the fabric, but each dress I made from a particular pattern would still look very similar. None, or at least very few, of my patterns are what you would call classics.

As a result, a large part of my collection looks dated. In fact, I have gotten rid of some really old ones at garage sales. When I decide to sew something for myself, I nearly always have to buy a new pattern. Evidently I'm still using my sewing machine for experiments. Perhaps I'm still trying to figure out who I am and where I fit in the universe.

I'm not encouraging you to become a clotheshorse. In Zen, self-awareness is the journey, not the ultimate outcome. The foundation of Buddhism is the Four Noble Truths, usually expressed in some variation of these four statements: Life is suffering. Suffering is caused by selfishness. Selfishness can be overcome. There are eight keys or pathways to overcoming self-ishness/suffering. These pathways are:

1. Right understanding
2. Right purpose
3. Right speech
4. Right conduct
5. Right livelihood
6. Right effort
7. Right alertness
8. Right concentration

All eight are good subjects for meditation. Try writing each of them on a separate piece of paper. When you sew, take one with you and put it where you'll see it. Think about that particular key and how it might be represented in your sewing as well as other aspects of your life. The reason for putting it where you can see it is so you'll come back to that thought when your mind wanders—and it will. At least mine always does.

An increase in self-awareness should lead to an equal increase in selflessness. Enlightenment comes as the ego fades, causing the perception of a separation between ourselves and others to fade as well.

 Try This

Next time you start a stitchery project, consider the color chart a suggestion and choose colors you like instead. Or choose some fabric that you really like, even if it is not something you would normally wear. Make something for yourself out of it. A skirt or a blouse would allow you to combine your extreme fabric with something more like your usual look. If you don't think you would ever have the nerve to wear this fabric, make yourself a tote bag, pillow, or some other object that you can use or display. Enjoy the experience of sewing with your new fabric or unusual thread or yarn.

chapter three

A Time to Sew

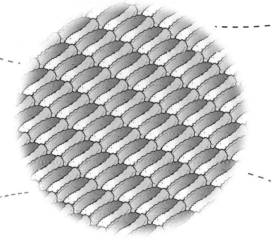

Tip: Needlework

To make your needlework look professional, be sure that your stitches are consistent. This means more than the size of the stitches. In cross-stitch, the top stitches of the X should all be in the same direction. In stem-stitch, the needle should always come up from the back stitch on the same side of the forward stitch. If you come up in the same hole as the last forward stitch, the back of your work will look almost the same as the front, a consideration when making something like tea towels. Satin stitches should run parallel to each other with no gaps between, but no overlapping either.

Making Home

We joke about it, but women actually do have a nesting instinct. Men may also, but it's usually overshadowed by some degree of a hunter/conquest kind of thing. They're happy to enjoy the comforts of the nest their women make for them, however.

While the nesting instinct may only become obvious in some women during the last few weeks before a baby is born, I suspect it is there all the time. Women, most of us anyway, love to decorate our space, and often that decorating includes needlecraft.

I was probably twelve or thirteen when I got a room of my own. The youngest of my parents' "first family" had left home for college when I was eight, but she came back most weekends for a few years. Eventually, she got all her stuff moved out and told Nora and me that, as long as she had a place to sleep when she came home, one of us could have her room. After some trading and moving of beds and dressers, I took possession of what had been Sally's room.

Almost immediately, I started nesting. I hemmed new curtains for the windows and new curtains for the "closet" which was actually a shelf with a rod suspended from it. I made pillows and covered nearly every horizontal surface with dresser scarves. It was way overdone, but it made the room mine. Oddly enough, though I liked to embroider and wouldn't have been afraid to try cross-stitch or needlepoint, I didn't stitch any pictures for the wall. I suppose I hadn't discovered those wonderful kits yet and their potential for decoration.

When I got married at twenty and moved in with my husband Joe, I set about doing the same thing again, with a little more sense of style, I hope. Most, if not all, of the curtains in the old farmhouse were ones left behind by my in-laws when they built their "new" house about ten years before.

I eventually made curtains for nearly every window in the house. As my family grew and the use of some rooms changed, I replaced curtains with more appropriate ones.

We added on to the house on three different occasions, shuffling room use even more. These major changes produced bursts of decorating energy. New curtains were called for (though I had some professionally made)—often tablecloths or placemats, pillows, crocheted doilies, or afghans as well.

To use a small example, when our oldest son was two, we enclosed a part of a porch to make a room for him on the ground floor. He seemed too young to be sent upstairs by himself and someone new was soon going to occupy the crib in the parlor. Jon's new room held (just barely) a crib-sized youth bed, a dresser, and a toy box. I made a bedspread with an appliquéd cowboy and curtains to match.

Three years later, he traded up and Eden got the tiny room, which called for new bedding to match the curtains. The youngest, Paul, bypassed the room by moving in with his brother, and the former piece of the porch became my sewing room for a short time. I made a small quilted mat to keep my sewing machine from scratching the surface of the mirrorless vanity table I refinished for a sewing desk. This mat matched the new curtains, of course.

After an addition gave me a larger sewing room (but one without windows, sad to say) the little room became a storage room. Sometime later I replaced the curtains again because they had faded. I should have learned by then to avoid cotton fabric on south-facing windows, but I didn't. The fabrics I like seem to be cottons more often than not, and cotton needs some synthetic fibers to keep it from sun-fading so quickly. These new curtains have faded again. For about a year now I've been fighting the urge to replace them. What's appropriate for a storage room that sits just off the dining room? Something with an old general store print, maybe? I could always go with flowers again. It's difficult for me to avoid those cotton prints.

Lately there's been some talk of replacing the window itself with the bay type, giving me a place for my plants. How would I want to do the curtains for something like that? And will I be able to wait until we've made the decision one way or another before those faded flowers I see every day get the better of me and I have to replace them anyway?

Feng Shui

As you can see, I'm still nesting. My family's needs changed as the children grew and will continue to change. My husband's and my jobs have changed, inside and outside of the household. New interests and hobbies need to be accommodated. As a result, I'm still making things, redecorating, and replacing.

While there have been large remodeling jobs, most of the changes have been little things, here or there. Lately, as I've made changes, I've tried to take feng shui into account. Feng shui, which literally means wind and water, is an ancient Chinese concept that seeks to promote harmony within an environment. It is applied to gardens and to dwelling space, such as the placement of a house on a lot, the arrangement of the rooms within the house, and the arrangement of items within each room. It is most closely related to Taoism, but also with Buddhism, which is usually associated with Zen. Taoism, Buddhism, and Confucianism make up the Three Ways of Eastern philosophy.

Feng shui offers a lot of suggestions for the placement of furniture and the like to ensure good ch'i, the energy that promotes the health and good fortune of the occupants. Some of the ideas seem strange to the Western mind, but others are very logical. Clutter, for one thing, should be kept to a minimum. An overabundance of items can block ch'i as well as symbolize too much clutter in our lives. The few items left on display after the rest are stored away are more attractive. Those things that we choose to leave out are probably the most significant to us in some way. Making the choices then taking a moment to discover our reasons can be enlightening.

Somewhere you'll find a balance between strict neatness and cluttered messiness. At that point your surroundings will feel welcoming and your creativity will flow more freely.

Applied to a sewing room, reduced clutter spells more efficiency. Projects that are started and not completed should be either finished or labeled and stored away until the mood is right to work on them. Storing tools close at hand reduces search time. I bought an extra pair of sewing shears because I was using my only pair at two different places in my sewing room and when I reached for them, they were always at the other place.

For better ch'i, you shouldn't have to work, either at your desk, stove, or sewing machine, with your back to the door. You'll be tense, always feeling as if someone could sneak up behind you. If you can't rearrange the furniture, a mirror hung appropriately can solve the problem.

If you want to sew but your sewing room isn't producing good vibrations for you, you might check out a book on feng shui from your local library. If nothing else, it might give you an excuse to make something new, such as a bright-colored table covering to put in some specific area of a room to enhance a particular aspect of your life.

I recently replaced the curtains in my office. I hated the old ones and they were right where I had to look at them when I worked at my computer. I found some very silky, almost sheer fabric with subdued red roses on a black background. They hang in a west window, and for once I thought to avoid cotton.

It was not easy fabric to work with, but the end product was worth it. They drape very gracefully when I tie them back, and they incorporate a little of the prescribed red into the Fame section of the room, though I haven't noticed that I'm more famous than I was. As I write this, my *Zen and the Art of Quilting* is being released. Maybe it and this book will make me famous, though I have to admit that desire for fame isn't particularly Zen anyway. At the very least, the new curtains keep the black blinds from looking like a mistake. The blinds are left from when the room belonged to Paul and were the only ones we could find that went with his camouflage curtains. I'm grateful we couldn't find any olive green or that's what I would have had to decorate around.

Fun by the Yard

I didn't really need new curtains, but I'm glad I made them. I've noticed with a lot of my sewing projects over the years, and especially the most recent ones, I'm more likely to find a need for something I want to make than to decide I want to make something I've noticed a need for.

It wasn't true in the case of my new office curtains, but often I find it's the fabric that suggests a project. I will see a pretty print or a particular color and think how it would go well some where in my house, much like another woman might see a vase or basket or china figure and imagine it in her home.

Sometimes the fabric doesn't even suggest anything in particular; it simply calls to me. My friend Nancy Collins has the same habit of buying fabric without a clear idea of what it might be used for. At least Nancy watches for sales.

In fact, it's possible that my thing for fabric is a large part of the reason I like to sew. I love to wander around in fabric stores, the larger the better. The largest one in my area that I've discovered is in the mid-sized town of McPherson, Kansas, about seventy miles from my home. It's called The Button Hole and has been written about in at least one quilting magazine. The fabrics they offer are predominately cottons, quilters' fabric of choice, but they offer other fabrics as well.

Seventy miles seems a little far for a shopping spree, so about a year went by after I first began hearing about the store before I got the chance to go there. My husband Joe had a need to head in that general direction and we decided to make a day of it. When we walked into the well-lit, beautifully decorated store, my husband took one look around and said, "You're going to be here awhile."

Yep. I sent him off to explore the rest of the town. He gave me an hour, which was barely enough. But if I hadn't been ready when he got back, he could have waited for me in the adjoining coffee shop, a great idea that other fabric stores ought to consider.

Of course, I don't need a huge fabric store to have fun. I'm about as likely to find a fabric I must have in Country Cousins in my home town or even in the fabric departments in the discount stores. I have planned entire quilts around fabrics I've noticed in these smaller stores. By the time I have a use for these fabrics, occasionally years later, their rivals in the store are forgotten. Now they are each compared with others in my stash, one among other favorites. Everything is relative.

The More Things Change

Zen masters often teach using koans, symbolic paradoxes that express an essential truth. Literally, koan means public record and refers to the recorded exchanges between teacher and student. One such koan is "Form is emptiness; emptiness is form." At first glance, this seems like nonsense, but essentially it is the recognition of the oneness of all things, or "forms," and yet the uniqueness of each. In our homes, emptiness (open space) becomes a sort of form. In our lives, emptiness might be understood as the quiet times as opposed to the busier times, or as the space left by loss, either an individual or a job or some other phase of our lives. That loss itself becomes a part of our current existence. For Zen masters, it means emptying ourselves of our selfness and seeing ourselves as a unique part of the whole. A related koan states, "Nothing exists essentially; nothing exists eternally."

We can use a decorated room to illustrate these principles. At a particular point in time around 1980, my relatively new couch was a separate unique form. So was each curtain and valance I made to match the background of the floral print fabric that covered the couch, and my very first ripple afghan. However, these items along with a few other pieces of furniture, the yellow sculpted carpet, and the old light fixture that hung in the center of the room made up my living room, as did the open space, the emptiness in the center of the room where my children played.

Taken a step further, the curtains themselves could be separated into warp and weft threads, individual fabric fibers—even into the molecules that made up the fibers. Nothing exists essentially but everything can be broken into ever smaller parts.

In the other direction, my living room was part of my whole house, part of the farm, part of the county, state, country, continent, world, universe. The idea is that all things (and all people) are interconnected. Conflict arises when we don't recognize this interdependence and try to protect some "form" from the forms around it as if they were separate.

To put this on an individual level, I tried to protect the curtains from small hands holding ice-cream bars. I tried to confine eating to the kitchen and dining room and tried a little to discourage the children from handling the curtains when they looked out the window. However, the living room window was one of the few in the house that was low enough for toddlers to see out of, and it was their house, too.

Keeping the curtains in perfect condition would have caused some family conflict. The curtains wore out eventually, as curtains do—not from smeared treats, but from time, the sun, and their own weight. I got tired of them long before that anyway. What had seemed like a nice neutral shade eventually started to look incredibly bland.

This brings us to the second point of this Zen principle. Nothing exists eternally. All these unique individual parts of the total oneness of all things are actually temporary. The current form they take at this moment in space and time is actually fluid. This includes us, of course. A lot of suffering comes when we fail to recognize this fact.

Take my curtains as an example again. I believe they were either cotton or linen, which means they had once been part of a plant. Before that they were seeds and before that part of their parent plant, etc. The plants were harvested, processed, spun, woven, dyed, shipped to a store, cut, stitched, and hung in front of my windows. Why should I assume that all this changing would suddenly stop?

And, of course, it didn't. The weight of the curtains pulled at the upper hems; the fabric frayed; and, like the child's room/storage room curtains, the sun faded the cream color to nearly white in places.

I've replaced them at least three times since then. I remember them as part of that fleeting moment when I was a young mother. They were part of that nest I made for my family.

If I had had limitless resources, I could have hired someone to decorate our home and make it look exactly like I wanted it to. However, there was and is more ownership and probably more homey-ness in the curtains I made, along with a pillow or two and the afghan, to coordinate with our one new piece of furniture, that floral couch. And that perfectly decorated room would have been just as temporary.

The More They Stay the Same

It seems it has always been true that women have the largest responsibility for the comforts of home. Cloth and thread and yarn and the things that she can turn them into are a large part of that comfort. Admittedly, technological changes have a profound effect on how we spend our time. Women's expectations, at least in developed countries, are much different now than they were even a generation ago. But that desire for home endures.

In Europe, from antiquity through the Middle Ages, women were the ones responsible for cloth production. In fact, the word "wife" may be derived from the same word as "weave." The work was similar in different regions, even though the materials the women had to work with varied. In ancient Egypt, they spun and wove flax into linen. In Mesopotamia, they used wool. The Chinese made silk. These ancient clothes were shapeless robes, which wrapped or draped around the wearer.

The ancient Persians in what is now Iran were the first among their neighbors to make fitted garments. They were horsemen and the fitted garments made riding easier. However, these garments were skins. Weaving came later for them.

At the same time that the people of Greece were fastening a rectangular piece of cloth at one shoulder and belting it in at the waist, eighty miles to the south on the Island of Crete, the women were making tight-waisted, bell-shaped skirts with wide ruffles that remind us of the European styles of the 1800s.

The Romans' clothing evolved from the Greeks and became the tunics and togas we associate with Roman senators. The Romans were the first to develop an extensive trade in textiles, importing silk from China, wool from England, and cotton from Egypt. The spread of the Roman Empire greatly influenced textiles and clothing styles in all of Europe.

When Rome fell in the A.D. 400s, trade diminished in all of their extensive holdings. England, Europe, and the new Byzantine Empire developed independently again. Women continued to make clothing as they had for hundreds of years, using what was available. In Western Europe, people blended the old Roman styles with furs and leather.

Around A.D. 1400, towns were growing and specialty shops began to appear, including businesses run by weavers and tailors. The quality of cloth and garments improved with the competition. Peasants' garments were still simple enough that untrained housewives could make them, while the garments for the wealthy became more elaborate and increasingly decorated with embroidery. At the same time, weaving became a male occupation because expanding trade made cloth production profitable. Some two hundred years later, European colonists to North America were among the purchasers of European cloth, even though some weavers immigrated. Restrictions on trade imposed by England prevented the colonists from exporting the cloth they produced. Cloth production in the colonies, therefore, was intended to supplement the imports from England. That severely limited the profits, and the responsibilities of cloth production shifted back to women.

The shift was gradual, of course. Women didn't get off the boats knowing how to weave. Most of them knew or quickly learned how to spin, however. Men who had been weavers in the old country could be hired to turn that homespun yarn into cloth. This piecemeal work was not especially lucrative and kept the men from pursuing more profitable enterprises, such as furniture-making or farming. They taught their wives, daughters, and neighbor women, who taught others, and so on.

In one county in Massachusetts which happened to take a census of such things, there was a threefold increase in household

looms between 1700, when 6 percent of the households owned
looms, and 1730. Both censuses showed that about one-half of
the households owned spinning wheels. Some places showed
closer to two-thirds at about the same time.

In diaries and household account books, women of the time
listed their production in spinning and weaving as household
activities along with knitting or soap-making. Unfortunately, at
the same time, weaving lost its artisan status. It was now housework rather than a respected profession. Homespun did not necessarily mean an inferior cloth, however. Skilled spinners made a
very fine, even thread that was woven into high quality cloth.

Ironically, modern fabric labeled "homespun" is a relatively
loose-woven cotton, often in earth-tone plaids, that is woven
from threads much heavier than colonists would have spun. And
most of what you'll find is made in India.

At any rate, young girls spun, wove, bleached, and hemmed,
and often embroidered tablecloths, napkins, and bed linens to
take with them when they married. A woman's wealth might be
measured in her bed and table linens. At a time when a woman's
possessions were considered her father's property and then her
husband's, diaries and account books reveal that often what a
woman sewed for her home, or future home, was considered
her own. In fact, sometimes she was allowed to trade her homespun for other goods for herself.

A chest the size of a small sideboard was sometimes given to
a girl as she was nearing marriageable age. These were where
the table linens and a few other personal items would be stored.
We know that they were given to unmarried girls who took them

with them when they married, because often they were decorated with the woman's first and maiden names or her initials
and were passed on later to her daughter along with the finest
of the linens.

Unfortunately, this wasn't the case in all households. In
some, the cloth that the wife and daughters wove from the flax
or wool or cotton that the husband raised was still considered
his. This is clear in some account entries where the sale of cloth
is listed along with other farm produce. I can't imagine my
husband claiming my quilts or other sewn projects as his own
and selling them. Saying that expectations were different then
doesn't really cover it. I'd guess that there was some resentment on the women's part. But there was resentment on the
man's part if he discovered, after marriage, that his wife couldn't
spin or weave as he had been led to believe. There is at least
one account of a man using that as grounds for divorce. He
claimed her friends hung hanks of yarn around in her house as
if they were her own intentionally to deceive him. Women were
expected to earn their keep.

England restricted more than the export of cloth from the
colonies. Cotton production was outlawed in an effort to protect the flax-growers and linen-producers of England. Laws that
forbade the import of cotton to England or the colonies were
imposed but soon repealed in favor of a tax on cotton. While
men discussed revolution, women increased their spinning
and weaving to decrease their dependence on imported cloth.
Spinning demonstrations and contests were written up in local
papers as patriotic displays.

Then Came the Revolution

The equipment used to manufacture textiles changed very little from the Middle Ages to the late eighteenth century. In 1764, James Hargreaves, an English weaver, invented a spinning machine that could spin many threads at once. Ten years later, Samuel Crompton, another English weaver, developed a spinning machine that could do as much as 200 spinners could by hand. I hate to think that men had to take over the production of textiles for it to see any major improvements, but perhaps men are more likely to think about big production while a woman's thoughts center more on her family.

There is some evidence, however, that Catherine Littlefield Greene may have actually been the one who invented the first efficient cotton gin. Eli Whitney was living with the widow while he attended law school. Women couldn't hold patents at the time, so this one was taken out in his name. They later married. At least that's the way revisionists tell it. He did go on to invent or improve equipment for manufacturing guns, so who knows who really invented the cotton gin. Perhaps it was a joint effort.

At any rate, innovations such as the cotton gin and the Jacquard loom, which could weave complex patterns, contributed to the Industrial Revolution. At the beginning of the nineteenth century, 75 percent of all clothing was still sewn at home. A century later, the amount of home sewing depended on location and economic circumstances.

Elinor Pruitt Stewart homesteaded in Wyoming in 1909. Her letters to her former employer in Denver, Colorado, are compiled in *Letters of a Woman Homesteader* (Boston: Houghton Mifflin, 1914). In one letter, she mentions that her husband gave her two dresses for Christmas, then immediately clarifies that in the box was material to make two dresses.

For most urban people, cloth production had moved from the home and into the factory. So what did women do with all this free time? Some went to work in the factories. But even if home spinning and weaving became an oddity, sewing was still a skill handed down from mother to daughter. In the mid-1800s, Elias Howe invented a sewing machine for factory use. A few years later, Isaac Singer developed a sewing machine for home use and quickly became rich enough to retire. Evidently a lot of women were eager for the time- and effort-saving machine. Many accounts of the time mention the excitement in the neighborhood when the first woman there got one. They also often mention how noisy the machines were.

Singer's wasn't the only treadle-powered sewing machine on the market, however. Raymond, Wheeler & Wilson, Weed, and Grovner-Baker machines were also on the market. All of them exaggerated their laborsaving capabilities in their ads. Women eventually discovered that the new, more complicated fashions that were made possible by the machines took nearly as much time as the simpler styles had by hand. Whether this was a disappointment or not, it's hard to guess. They didn't rebel en mass and bring back the earlier styles. I suspect many women liked the new styles and felt they were worth the extra effort.

At about the same time, patterns were beginning to appear in ladies' magazines such as *Godey's Lady's Book* and *Harper's*

Bazaar. Without patterns, women dismantled worn-out clothes and used the pieces as patterns or made their own by measure.

In rural areas and especially on the frontier, a young woman would accumulate quilts in her hope chest rather than tablecloths of a century before. She was expected to make a dozen quilts before she became engaged and one more, a special bride quilt, before the wedding. These quilts would set her up in housekeeping, but wouldn't last forever. She'd have to keep quilting as her family grew and the old quilts wore out.

Early settlers on the plains lived in sod houses or dugouts. Logs were simply not available the way they had been for the early settlers farther east. Turning what amounted to mud huts into homes was the first priority of the women. Besides the hand-stitched sampler on the wall, curtains seem to be a near-universal symbol of civilization to them. They fashioned curtains out of what they had: muslin, old sheets, cheesecloth, canvas from their covered wagons, and even newspapers. Often there was no glass in these windows they were framing. Oiled cloth or even paper let in air and light and filtered out dust and insects. These windows must have looked incongruous with lace curtains saved from the former home hung in front of them.

In 1835, Sophia Suttenfield Auginbaugh moved to the wilds of Texas, where her husband abandoned her. Four years later she was granted a divorce from her absent husband and married Holland Coffee, who ran a trading post at Preston Bend. Her story is told in an article by David Jennys in the February 1998 issue of *Wild West* titled "In the Red River region, merchant Holland Coffee tasted the full flavor of the frontier."

Sophia and Holland had a lapboard house with a puncheon floor, which would probably have been made from split logs. A dry goods box nailed to the wall served as a wardrobe and another with legs made the table. They lived there for ten years. Much later, Sophia wrote, "The first quilt I made in Grayson County I picked the cotton out of our field with my own fingers, Col. Coffee placed the quilt out in squares and I quilted it." The cotton she picked would have been used for batting, and this is what her husband helped her lay out after it had been carded.

She goes on to say, "I then made a rag carpet . . . Viewing my quilt, wardrobe and puncheon carpet I was the happiest woman in Texas." Perhaps it didn't take much to make her happy. Sometimes I think that the more we have the more we want. We might also argue that time had tinted her memory, making her life seem a bit rosier than it had been. In the same letters, however, she describes making coffee late at night for her husband and others who had come to the trading post for shelter when they feared an Indian attack, certainly not a rosy picture.

In later years she may have looked back on how her creative efforts, illustrated by a quilt and a rug, made a vast difference in the appearance and comfort of her home. In a more affluent time and "civilized" place, those same efforts might have seemed quaint at best.

There's also the possibility that the quilt and the rug symbolized the happiness she felt, rather than causing it.

On the trails and in the dirty fields, there was no need for elegant fabrics or high-fashion styles. Clothing on the frontier was simple, practical, and economical. The men wore denim or canvas pants and heavy homespun shirts. Women usually had two dresses. They tried to save one as a good dress. Often, at first, that dress was one brought West with them. Once it wore out, a new calico dress was good enough. Sunbonnets and muslin aprons rounded out a woman's wardrobe.

On the plains, women often cut a few inches off the bottom of their dresses to make walking through tall grass, not to mention plowing a field or hoeing a garden, much easier. They also put lead shot in the hems to keep their dresses from billowing in the wind. George Armstrong Custer is credited with this innovation—at least by his wife, who after his death made her living by writing about him.

Believe it or not, women in the West wore bloomers. These were named for Amelia Bloomer, a women's rights advocate who began wearing them in the early 1850s. These were baggy trousers that gathered at the ankle and were worn beneath a tunic-style dress. A Kansas pioneer woman Miriam Davis Colt wrote in 1856 that they were well suited to her life on the plains, making walking through the tall grass easier and decreasing the chances of catching her clothes on fire. Brigham Young, the Mormon leader, advocated the bloomers for overland travelers but not for wear once the settlers reached their home in Utah.

But women didn't come to the wilderness to live in a primitive fashion, even if different clothes actually suited their environment. They came to transplant civilization to the wild frontier. The homespun and sunbonnets gave way to the fashions of the East as soon as it was economically possible.

In 1868, an unnamed woman writing for the Illinois State Agricultural Society advocated the professionalization of domestic labor. When a farm family had to choose between new labor-saving farm equipment and new household technologies, the field nearly always won over the home. The notion that only farm produce supported the family was faulty. The wife's contributions to the household in clothes, canned foods, homemade soap, and often small cash crops from chickens or even bees were simply never tallied like her husband's field crops. She was ignored. While circumstances may be very different today, I don't believe that women's contributions in childrearing and home management are valued nearly as much as her paycheck. Maybe as we learn to value our own contributions more, others will as well.

Creative License

Whether we feel like it's an important contribution to our family's lifestyle or a guilty pleasure, many of us keep right on crafting things for our homes. There are basically two types of things that we nesters like to make, things that are functional and things that are intended simply to decorate. Our favorites are the things that do both. In fact, nearly all of the functional things we make are as beautiful as our resources and skills will allow. I suspect this is part of the reason quilting is so popular now. What could better symbolize a nest than a beautiful, warm, handmade quilt?

Curtains can work somewhat the same way. They provide privacy and are sometimes a dramatic complement to the colors in the room. They are also a good project for beginning sewers because they are easy to make. More experienced sewers like to make more complicated styles.

The living room curtains that I made shortly after I was married seemed relatively plain, but I had to put crinoline in the top hem and pleat them to make them hang the way I wanted them to. Both of these techniques were new to me. I was a little stingy with the hem allowance at the top, and that, combined with the loose weave of the fabric, caused the top hems to pull out. Still, I learned a lot from making them, and they functioned well for a number of years.

Things that are made purely as art have a special significance, but we are often afraid to try them. If something functional doesn't turn out just like we imagined it, we can always console ourselves by saying that it will still serve its purpose. But a piece of art that doesn't look right to the artist seems like a failure. Also, many of us feel guilty about the time and expense involved in making something that doesn't seem to do anything.

I say *seem* because art always *does* something. It attracts us or repels us, soothes us or intrigues us. Even if it bores us, that's a reaction of sorts. Art rarely looks exactly like it was envisioned anyway. That's part of the fun of making art, and part of the danger.

All those cross-stitch, needlepoint, and crewel kits qualify as art, even if they aren't exactly original. And if we turn them into pillow tops instead of framing them, they are still primarily decorative rather than functional. My first attempt at fabric art was a crewel kit with an orange sun setting behind bare tree trunks and branches. The fabric was burlap, which turned out to be more difficult to work with than I expected. I stitched away on the tree trunks rather quickly.

The sun was a different matter. The pattern called for red and orange circles of chain stitches that alternated directions. I don't know if I didn't notice the change of direction or if I thought I'd do it the easy way, but I stitched away in one continuous spiraling chain of stitches. Unfortunately, this stretched the fabric, causing the sun to puff out between the trees. The entire kit was abruptly stored away. Its lack of beauty had ruined all its value.

Years later I got it out, took out all the red chain stitches, steam-pressed it—and put it back in storage. In reality the sun was only half the problem. When I started it, I thought I was going to have a perfect place to hang it. Our remodeling plans changed, destroying my incentive to finish the project. Now I have a quilt hanger on the living room wall, and I keep wondering if those silhouetted trees wouldn't look great hanging from it in the autumn. It would probably be better backed with fabric and hung as a wall hanging rather than framed anyway. Some day it'll call to me, and I'll set something else aside to finish it.

One step beyond a wall hanging is the soft sculpture. Or perhaps "soft sculpture" is simply a name given to certain wall hangings so that artsy types will know they are art. I define the difference between a fabric wall hanging and a soft sculpture by depth. Most wall hangings are flat or nearly so. Soft sculpture includes different weights of fabric or pieces of fabric placed in such a way that the hanging has three dimensions. For example, I made a watercolor quilt that I hang on the wall. I consider it art but not soft sculpture. However, my definition isn't perfect because by it you could say that a stuffed toy is soft sculpture. Maybe that's not a bad idea.

Perhaps art is in the eye of the beholder or the mind of the artist. If you choose to use a fabric construction to decorate your living room, it's art, whether it's a quilt or a stuffed rabbit. If you tuck that same object into bed with a child, it's probably not art, though it may be just as wonderful.

At any rate, you shouldn't feel guilty about making something you don't plan to use except for decoration. Artistic endeavors may actually help us understand the concepts of form and emptiness better than functional items. For one element to stand out in our work of art, something else must be more subdued or placed in the background. The appearance of both of these elements is altered by what surrounds it, sometimes in surprising ways. Each element is unique, yet part of the whole.

Imagine yourself as one element in a soft sculpture. You need to fully realize and fulfill your true nature or purpose in this sculpture (world). At the same time, you need to realize that you are not separate from the whole but, as the Zen masters say, "one of the ten thousand things" that make up the universe. The equal recognition of these two ideas is enlightenment.

 Try This

Make something purely for decoration. If you are new to sewing, make a covering for an accent table. If you've done more
sewing, make a wall hanging. If you've made wall hangings
before, make something more elaborate, add different types of
cloth, vary the texture and the depth, and call it a soft sculpture. If you like handwork, pick out a cross-stitch pattern or kit
because you like it, not because it goes with anything. Or see
if you can design your own. Let your imagination guide you,
and pay attention to what you learn.

chapter four

The Thread That Binds

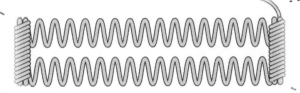

Tip: Pattern Storage

If you are accumulating quite a few clothing patterns, you need to organize them so you can find what you're looking for. One suggestion is to make a notebook for the empty envelopes, using clear plastic page protectors. Arrange the envelopes into categories that make sense to you. Store the pattern pieces themselves, along with the directions, in manila envelopes. This solves the problem of refolding the patterns to fit the tiny envelopes. Print the pattern number clearly on the outside of the manila envelopes and file them in numerical order in a file box or drawer. You can look through your notebook, pick the pattern you want to use, then find the pieces easily in your file box.

Sewing Sister Dresses

When we were growing up, Nora and I wore look-alike outfits that our mother called "sister" clothes. I remember dresses, short sets, even flannel shirts and jeans that matched. They weren't "twin" dresses because we weren't twins, you see, and they were usually the same pattern made in different colors. Dark-haired, brown-eyed Nora was usually in red or pink, and I was in blue to match my eyes. At the time, I wanted to wear pink, which helps explain why it's a favorite today.

Mom may have made some of the outfits. I know she hemmed them, often several times. The dresses would start out with deep, deep hems. By the time we outgrew them the bottom few inches were striped with old creases. She stitched a round of grosgrain ribbon to the bottom edge of the dress to serve as a hem allowance, turned it under, and hemmed it.

To this day, when I see two fabrics that look alike except for their color, especially if they are tiny flower prints, I feel nostalgic. Oddly enough, the only dresses I actually remember precisely were red and blue plaid with red trim. Nora's and mine were of the same fabric. We told them apart because the cuff of mine had been cut on the blue section of the plaid and Nora's had been cut on the red, and because by then Nora's was about 3" longer than mine. The memory is reinforced by a photograph. There had to have been some little flower dresses, though, or I wouldn't feel so drawn to those fabrics.

For a few years I found a way to give that bittersweet inclination some expression. Nora gave birth to a dark-haired girl about six months before my blue-eyed blond daughter was born. When Nora brought her family from Illinois to Kansas to visit each summer and occasionally at Christmas time as well, I would try to have cousin dresses or cousin tops for our two little girls.

I may have only done it three or four times. Eden had a strong sense of identity at a surprisingly early age and didn't want anyone else to dress like her. I had to talk her into allowing it for one day, promising her that Tanya would go back home and then nobody would be dressed like her anymore.

Nora's Kevin and my Paul are less than a year apart, too. I think I made matching clothes for them once, but it wasn't the same. While I enjoyed sewing for my boys, it didn't give me the chance to relive my childhood the way sewing sister dresses did.

Besides, little girls are wonderfully fun to sew for. When Eden was small I could go nuts with ruffles and lace. I even smocked one dress, and I remember a little toddler dress that had $35 worth of lace on it. Clearly I wasn't always saving money by sewing.

What I enjoyed about sewing for my children had more to do with the children themselves than the clothes I could add to their closet. It's nearly impossible to sew for someone and not think about that person as you sew.

Midnight Oil

Part of Proverbs 31 in the Bible describes a capable wife. About one-fourth of the descriptions in the twenty-two verses have to do with clothing and clothing production. "She seeks wool and flax and works with willing hands . . . She puts her hands to the distaff (the staff for holding the flax during spinning) and her hands hold the spindle . . . She is not afraid for her household when it snows for all her household are clothed in crimson. She makes herself coverings, her clothing is fine linen and purple . . . She makes linen garments and sells them . . . Strength and dignity are her clothing." On top of all this, verse 18b says, "Her lamp does not go out at night" (New Revised Standard Version).

Several women I talked to related times when they had stayed up late finishing something for some member of their family. Birthday and Christmas gifts that were intended as surprises were almost always stitched only after everyone else was in bed. I remember look-alike pajamas for my two sons and their father that were finished in the early hours of Christmas morning. More recently I knitted each of my children sweaters, increasing my pace and staying up later and later as the deadline approached.

My 4-H leader, Mariesther Holbert, remembers staying up until past midnight finishing an outfit one daughter needed for the 4-H style review the next day after spending the day at the hospital with the other daughter, who had been in a car accident.

Neither of us was up quite all night, but it happens. Way back in my mother's family history there lived a woman named Harriet Skinner Burton. She was born in 1805 in Norwick, New York. Orphaned at twelve and married at sixteen, she was the mother of ten children, eight of whom lived to adulthood. She and her husband Hiram farmed near the shores of Lake Erie. Besides farming, Hiram was a builder. He knew how to build with brick and stone, logs and lumber. He built everything from houses to bridges to chairs and bureaus. He was also an expert tailor.

Hiram and Harriet owned a spinning wheel—perhaps more than one—and a loom. Harriet sewed and knitted almost all of the family's clothes from thread, yarn, and cloth that she and her children made. Hiram would cut out a garment and Harriet would stitch it, and the family liked to joke that sometimes she would finish before he did.

When her second child, Linus, was probably still in his teens, he had an opportunity to teach penmanship. Since people didn't commute the way they do now, this required a move into town. His older brother, named Hiram after their father, wrote years later, "mother learned that Linus intended to go away from home the next morning." Either the offer was a very sudden one or Linus kept his plan a secret from his mother as long as possible. The latter possibility would give us a clue to his youth.

Harriet waited until the rest of the family had all gone to bed, then she went through her son's packed trunk. I would imagine that most mothers have done that, or at least wanted to. To preserve our children's privacy, we will usually settle for the verbal "did-you-remember-to-pack . . . " list.

When Harriet examined the contents of the trunk she determined that Linus needed a pair of pants. Staying up all night, she cut out a pair and stitched them by hand. She had them packed in the trunk before the family got up in the morning.

Young Hiram's account of this incident is brief, two run-on sentences, but we learn a great deal about Harriet from it.

She could sew quickly by lamplight, and she had a length of appropriate cloth on hand. We don't know if that cloth had been intended for something else, which she decided was less important, or if she always had some cloth ahead. This says a little about the affluence of the family.

We also learn that Harriet was willing to sacrifice a night's sleep for her son. We don't know Linus's reaction, though the older brother was impressed enough to write about it later. We also don't know how old Linus was, but my guess is around fifteen. A grade school education qualified you to teach in most elementary-level schools. A family history compiled by a younger brother, Charles, states that all the "children completed the common school courses and had some further education in Fredonia Academy." The academy may have been similar to high school, so Linus could still have been quite young. It must have been difficult for Harriet to let him go.

With the amount of work everyone did in those days, a night's sleep was no small thing to sacrifice. Besides the three boys who were within five years of each other in age, there was a boy eight years younger than Linus and two children eleven years younger. Harriet's sister had died four days after giving birth to a daughter, and Harriet and her husband were raising the girl, who was close to the same age as their fifth son. Harriet had her next child when Linus was seventeen, but I doubt if he was that old yet when she stayed up to make the pants.

At any rate, Harriet had plenty of work to do the next day. Young children require energy and patience, both of which would have been difficult to muster after a sleepless night. We don't know how Linus felt about his mother's sacrifice. He had not asked her to stay up all night, nor even mentioned his shortage of clothes. He probably marveled that his mother thought the pants were worth losing sleep over.

The truth of the matter is, the pants probably weren't. But Linus was. Harriet might have reasoned that she wouldn't have slept anyway for worrying about her son. By staying up, she put action to her concern. She may have even felt compelled to do it. I'm sure she felt better about his going because of her efforts. And what do you suppose occupied her mind all night as she sewed? I imagine she shed a tear or two as she accepted the fact that her child was growing up and leaving the nest. Nowhere is there any indication that she tried to stop him. She probably felt more as if she was sacrificing her son to the world than a night's sleep for her son.

The story of Hannah, who made a coat for her son every year, comes to mind. The story is found in First Samuel of the Bible and is a strange story in some ways. Hannah is one of two wives of Elkanah. The other wife, Peninnah, had children and would torment Hannah because she had none. Year after year Hannah prayed for a son. Finally she promised to dedicate her son to God if her prayers were answered. When they were, she kept her promise, bringing Samuel to the temple once he was weaned. He was probably three or four years old when she left him in the priest Eli's care.

The temple was far enough away from Hannah's home that she couldn't see her son often, but every year she and her husband made a pilgrimage to the temple, and she would always bring him a new coat or shirt she had made.

Our modern sensibilities are a little shocked by the implications of this story. This oldest child (he had five younger brothers and sisters) would be expected to have abandonment issues. A coat would hardly make up for it.

But those were different times and a different culture. Hannah saw her act of sacrifice as service to God. Children were expected to do what their parents told them to do. Children not much older than Samuel might have been apprenticed out to skilled workers of one kind or another. Choosing your child's occupation (or spouse) was not looked upon as high-handed, as it is today. Hannah was certain she had done what God wanted her to do. The proof was in the fact that she had more children after sacrificing, in a sense, her firstborn. The coat she made each year for her absent son would have been stitched with bittersweet tenderness.

See What Fits

Nowadays, it's sometimes the children who think they are making the sacrifice by wearing clothes that their mother or grandmother has made for them. The seamstress wants the clothes to fit; the child wants clothes that let them fit in. I think they agree very early with Polonius in Shakespeare's Hamlet when he says, "The apparel oft proclaims the man."

Karla McMillan told me that her daughter had the opposite reaction. She had been making most of Ashley's clothes, but when Wal-Mart opened in town, she bought her some cute outfits for school. Ashley came home from school and announced that she didn't want to wear the store-bought clothes again because other girls at school had some just like them. She didn't want to blend in *that* much.

My own children were willing to wear most of what I made, but they didn't actively encourage me to sew for them. They were afraid, on the one hand, that I would somehow mess up. I was old, you see, and couldn't possibly know what kids were wearing. On the other hand, if they did trust me to make something, they hated to wait for it. Sometimes, I'll admit, I got distracted with other projects and the garment they were waiting for took way too long. Also, they were used to picking out their own clothes and wanted to see what they were going to get. That wasn't entirely possible with clothes I was sewing until they were finished. It takes some practice to look at a picture and imagine it done up in a completely different fabric. Sometimes even experienced sewers are surprised. A friend of mine made up a dress for herself out of fabric that had a tiny red and blue print. These are the colors of the University of Kansas. Living in an area made up of more Kansas State University fans, she thought she was being very clever, discreetly displaying the colors of her preferred college. However, when you see the dress from a distance, the two colors blend together and look purple, Kansas State's color. She could laugh about it, but my kids might have refused to wear an outfit that played them such a trick.

By the time they were in the third or fourth grade, my kids would wear what I made only if it looked like it was store-bought. Since about all they wanted to wear were jeans and T-shirts, I made less and less for them as they grew older.

They were willing to wear the pajamas I made, however, since nobody saw them but us. I didn't realize how many pajamas I'd made for the oldest child until I put my finished (finally!) Cathedral Window quilt on the guest bed for Jon when he visited last summer. The quilt has lots and lots of 2" squares of different fabrics, and I used scraps left from projects that went back years. It was the fabrics left from his many different pajamas that he recognized.

My daughter, Eden, has been sewing some the last few years. Among her first efforts have been pajama pants for herself and close friends and a bathrobe for her boyfriend. (He's 6'7" tall, and a store-bought robe for him would have been expensive.) But the robe turned out to be a bit of a challenge. To accommodate his above-average height, she had to alter the pattern. Also, she couldn't understand the instructions for attaching the collar and for backing the lapel. She had to develop her own way to do it. "Kevin's fleece robe," she says, "wouldn't win any prizes at a fair, but it does the job and looks nice on him." She chooses these projects partly because she can be assured that there won't be as many people judging her sewing efforts.

Confidence needs a little time to develop when you're trying anything new. Pajama pants make excellent beginning projects because they are simple. After making a few from cotton, she tried rayon. It was a good chance to work with that tricky fabric, making something that didn't have to be perfect.

Sometimes, instead of finding something our loved ones will *let* us sew, we receive special requests that can't be met unless we sew them. I'm usually thrilled when my kids come to me with a request, but occasionally overwhelmed, as when Eden couldn't find the kind of prom dress she wanted. We found a pattern for a skirt and top that went with a sort of bustier piece she had found. We even found fabric that was just what she wanted—and that frayed faster than I could sew it. I didn't know about the liquid glue that you can use to treat the edges of your fabric. I just tried to be careful and finish the edges of every seam. The outfit had a bit of a Cinderella look, definitely unlike any other dress at the prom, but exactly what Eden wanted.

A couple of years ago my older son, Jon, came home to film a movie for his master's thesis. While he was still in the planning stages, he called and asked if I would be able to make all the costumes. When he auditioned the actors for the parts, I would take their measurements, a fellow student would design the costumes, and I would use these pictures and the measurements to make the costumes. I would have loved to help, but I didn't trust my tailoring skills to work without patterns. He was disappointed but found someone in New York to do the sewing for him. I did help on audition day with the measurements and did some last-minute altering on a couple of the costumes—I could handle that. When I saw the slapped-together workmanship and heard what Jon had had to pay for them, I really wished I could have taken on the project.

I was able to meet a couple of Jon's requests recently. He wanted an embroidered sampler that would look like an antique with a silly saying that no one would notice unless they really looked at it. I used a tan cloth and faded-looking thread to stitch the alphabet and numbers along with "We get our orders from

Moscow." He liked my finished piece so much that he requested a sampler for his wife with one of her favorite quotes. He didn't want it to be too ordinary, so I chose a counted cross-stitch pattern in the medallion fashion—that is, it had a symmetrical motif in the center surrounded by concentric motifs or borders. I stitched the quote, *"How perfectly goddamn delightful it all is, to be sure."—Charles Crumb*, on the next-to-last border, with the tops of all the letters away from the center. The person who framed it had trouble figuring out which way was up.

When we offer our family special features, we may get a job for life. Nancy Collins makes nearly all of her husband's shirts. He would have to shop at big and tall stores otherwise, but even apart from the convenience, he likes Nancy's shirts better—she puts in big breast pockets.

Jane Snavely, the neighbor who makes custom curtains for pay, also makes all of her husband's shirts. Armand lost an arm in an accident with a corn picker shortly after he was out of high school. After all these years of working with the artificial arm, his shoulders aren't the same size. Jane's shirts fit him better than anything he could buy. She also uses a double layer of fabric in one sleeve so the metal hinge doesn't wear through quite so quickly. You're not going to find anything like that in a store.

Sewing with Conviction

The first year Nancy Collins was in the Peace Corps, she lived in a house owned by a woman who sewed for her family, some of whom lived up in the mountains. They would send her their measurements, and she would make them clothes. Nancy sewed a lot and had grown up wearing clothes her mother made, but she was impressed with this woman's skill. If I could have taken lessons from the woman, I would have been able to make my son's costumes.

Later on, Nancy was given the use of a treadle machine owned by the Peace Corps. It took some getting used to, but she managed to do some sewing on it. Sometime after she returned to the States and her children were born, she decided that she wouldn't buy anything that she could sew or knit herself. Since she is quite accomplished in both areas, that includes nearly everything she wears and what her children wore as long as they were home. By the time she bought her children their first pairs of factory-made blue jeans, one was in high school and the other in junior high.

Sewing was always helpful economically, sometimes a clear necessity. Her children were more cooperative than most, perhaps because the rule was in place from the beginning. They voiced objections occasionally, however. Tad came home from his first day in kindergarten and announced that from then on his pants had to have zippers in them. Nancy had to quickly learn how to make fly fronts, even in pants with elastic in the waist.

Nancy's resolution to do as much of the family's sewing as possible grew in part from her social consciousness. Clothes she makes herself are not made with exploited labor. It also taught her children to postpone gratification and to plan ahead. They couldn't rush out and buy something as soon as they thought they needed it. As a result, they grew up more conscious of social issues than social status.

I'm sure Nancy never saw her sewing as a sacrifice, because she's always loved to sew. If she was sewing purely for the pleasure of it, however, she could have sewed only for herself. Instead she kept her two children and husband well dressed, as well as herself. Before she retired from teaching, she would sew like mad over the summer, then everything would sit from the beginning of the school year until Thanksgiving. The rest of the school year she managed to find a little time now and then to sew, but that transition from summer at home to the beginning of the school year always kept her too busy to sew.

I believe Nancy sees sewing as a bit of a calling, a talent and skill she is expected to use. First Corinthians 12 of the Bible speaks of the gifts of the spirit, those things that we are to share out of love. Another way to look at it is dharma. Dharma, sometimes translated as wisdom, can be defined as divine law. To follow divine law, you have to conform to your duty. To discover your duty, you first must discover your true nature or truest self, which is the whole point of Zen.

Usually what we love to do is where our talents lie. If we can turn those talents into service, our love of the task will keep it from feeling like a sacrifice. Besides, is there a better way to touch God than through loving service?

My favorite story of wise loving service involves a pair of overalls made, not for a child to wear, but for a teddy bear. When he was little, Nora's husband Jim had a beloved bear. He still has it, as a matter of fact. His children played with it when they were little. His sons thought it was pretty special because of the overalls, but his daughters were annoyed by the clothes. They were actually sewn onto the bear and couldn't be removed so the girls could change his outfit.

But back to Jim, or rather Jimmy. As a child, he took his then-naked bear with him everywhere he went. Jimmy especially liked to give his bear rides on his tricycle. One winter day, Jimmy's mother told him the bear was cold. Jimmy had nice warm overalls and his bear wanted some too. She made the bear some overalls that looked just like Jimmy's. She had probably made Jimmy's, too, and used the scraps for the bear's. They were so cleverly made that people commented on the bear's cute overalls.

This was after the Depression, but many farmers, including Jim's family, were still struggling to repay debts. At the time, Jimmy was one of five children including a baby. Two more children were born later. Jimmy's mother had plenty of people to sew for. She didn't decide to make the teddy bear some clothes just because she wanted a project. She was covering the holes on a bear that had been loved to pieces. She was extending the life of a beloved toy—rescuing it, really. But she did it by entering the child's world and saving his pride along with the bear.

Spin a Yarn

Hans Christian Andersen, who happened to be born the same year as my ancestor who stayed up all night to make her son's pants, wrote one of my favorite fairy tales. *The Wild Swans* is about a heroic seamstress who, like so many fairy tale heroines, was also a princess. The Brothers Grimm tell a more complicated version of the same story in *The Six Swans*. Their collected folk tales predate Andersen's by a few years, but I like Andersen's version better. Both stories were probably based on a folktale that went back further still.

As is true so often in fairy tales, there is an evil stepmother —two, in fact, in the Grimm version—but only Andersen gives the princess a name, Eliza. Eliza has eleven brothers who are turned into swans by their jealous stepmother. Eliza is driven from the castle and goes in search of her brothers. She finds them just as the sun is going down and watches them return to their human forms.

Eliza learns in a dream that only she can remove the curse. She must break open the stems of stinging nettle plants to make flax to spin and weave and sew into shirts for each brother. She cannot say a word until the spell is broken or her brothers will die.

Eliza sets to work immediately, even though the nettles burn blisters on her hands. Her brothers can't understand what she is doing nor why she won't speak to them. As the sun comes up, they resume their swan shapes and fly away.

While Eliza is sewing the second shirt, a young king finds her in the forest and falls in love with her beauty. He takes her back to his castle, but all she does is spin, weave, and sew. At night she leaves the castle to gather nettles from the graveyards.

This is enough to make the people of the kingdom, with some prompting from the bishop, decide that Eliza is a witch. The king reluctantly admits that this must be true since she won't explain herself, and our heroine is sentenced to be burned at the stake. As she rides in the wagon that is to take her to her death, she continues to work on the shirts.

The people are sure that the shirts hold some evil magic and rush the wagon, intending to rip them to pieces, but eleven swans alight on the cart, frightening the people away. Even as the executioner grabs her, Eliza throw the shirts over the swans and they turn into her brothers again. Unfortunately, only one sleeve was complete on the last shirt and the youngest brother has a swan's wing instead of a left arm. But now Eliza is able to tell her story and lives happily ever after with the king.

As a child, I worried about the youngest brother. I felt terrible for the seamstress who couldn't sew quite fast enough. I wanted another story that would tell how the last remnant of the curse was lifted. I was sure the young prince would accomplish some noble task and a real arm and a princess would be his reward. Maybe he found a woman like Jane who would sew him special shirts.

Eliza is a woman with a mission. She is going to make a shirt for each brother or die trying. She remained dedicated to her purpose, her dharma, through persecution and blistered fingers, more than most of us have been asked to endure.

But if your son is leaving in the morning and he needs another pair of pants, or if your child's teddy bear is in danger of disintegrating, you feel a little of Eliza's mission in your heart. You do the best you can, hoping the imperfections of your hurried creation won't stand out as obviously as a swan's wing.

Try This

Consider the needs of members of your family. Does someone need a garment you could sew? Does someone need to be encouraged with a small gift you can needlepoint? Is someone about to embark on an adventure such as college or a move to a new job away from home? Could you cross-stitch something that will remind that person of home and family? Or are you the one who is away from home? Stitch something for yourself that reminds you of your ties to the rest of your family.

chapter five

Stitch and Grow

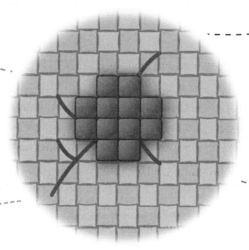

Tip: Labels

If you are stitching something to give away, write very brief care instructions on twill tape, seam binding, or ribbon with permanent ink or a Pigma pen intended for fabric and hide the ends in a seam somewhere. The "Made especially for you by . . ." labels are also nice but can be expensive. If you want your name on the craft forever, embroider it or write it with a Pigma pen. Needlecrafted pictures should have the stitcher's initials at the very least. Consider including the date as well.

On Needles and Pins

I love babies (most of us do), and I love all kinds of needlecrafts. Over the years, babies have given me excuses to make lots of things. When my own children were only a little past the infant-gown-and-rompers stage, I got a kick out of sewing these types of clothes for the babies of relatives and friends. In those days before the sex of a child was known well in advance of the birthday, I tried to have a little dress and a little overall set ready ahead. I tried to crochet a baby blanket or two ahead as well, in case I was invited to a shower before a baby was born.

As my own children got older, I worried that my baby patterns were getting old-fashioned. I relied more on knitting and crocheting for my baby gifts. Unless I had plenty of notice, however, it was hard for me to get a yarn project done before the baby was born, and I just couldn't seem to keep a blanket ahead. In the last few years, marathon crocheting has given me tendonitis in my forearm. There is a wealth of tempting needle-work pictures appropriate for a baby's room, but I hesitate to do someone else's decorating. As a consequence, I've gone back to sewing and have become enamored of quilting.

Because of the size, baby quilts go together pretty quickly. They aren't difficult to machine-quilt, but if I want to hand-quilt one for someone special, they are small enough to quilt on a lap or hand-held hoop and will travel well to waiting rooms or on vacation. Baby quilts have the added advantage of being lightweight and unbreakable, making them easy to mail. In fact, I think they are the perfect baby gift. I wish I had discovered them sooner.

Granted, buying fabric, cutting it up, and sewing the pieces back together doesn't make much sense to the nonquilter. Unless I'm using fabric scraps left from other projects, I'm probably not saving any money, either. But how many handmade gifts do new parents get these days? With a quilt, there's no danger of them receiving another exactly like mine, and if they get something similar, that's all right. They can always use one more blanket.

That is only part of the reason I've started making baby quilts, though. I love looking through the wide selection of juvenile prints and choosing contrasting fabrics. I love deciding which should be dominant and which should be supporting, though sometimes I have to take into account how much of each fabric I have on hand when making those decisions.

I enjoy coming up with patterns that fit the amount of fabric I have or using old standard patterns in clever ways. I'm currently using the Bear's Paw pattern with some Winnie-the-Pooh fabric and I want to use up some farm animal print with Hole in the Barn Door. I realize that part of the fun will be lost on the recipient if she doesn't recognize the pattern, but I can enjoy it and feel clever while I sew. Quilts illustrate so wonderfully the principle of unity of all things. The small individual pieces create one unified whole, reminding me of the interdependence of all living beings. The patterns on the fabrics inside the related pattern of the blocks remind me of the changing nature of things, from the cottonseed onward. Buying a cotton quilt wouldn't be the same as constructing one, of course. It's the process of planning, cutting, and stitching that frees my creative and reflective spirit.

On a purely practical note, a machine-pieced, machine-quilted baby quilt can go together faster than a crocheted blanket with considerably less tendon strain. This is a good thing for me right now, because in the last five months I've learned of nine new babies born or due before the end of the year among family and friends. Five of the quilts are finished and delivered and three more, the Bear's Paw ones, are started. Actually, there's enough Pooh fabric for the ninth quilt as well, but I like the quilts so much that I'm going to save one to hand-quilt and put in my Grandma hope chest. I may wait until I've heard whether the last baby's a boy or a girl before I buy more fabric, in case I want to go with something overtly sexist. Besides, if I'm running late with a quilt, I can make it a little bigger and give it to the child when he's several months old. We don't outgrow our need for blankets.

Gone or Forgotten

There's something special about these quilts even though they don't stay in my possession very long. I live with them only for the time it takes me to put them together, then I relinquish them, often to a family that I don't really know well. Yet enough thought and labor has gone into even the quickest quilt that it feels familiar to me, and I recognize a danger of becoming attached to it.

With any gift, there seems to be a certain amount of tension when the time comes to give it up. Normally, my fear is not that the gift will be unappreciated. When I was younger, I might have worried that my sewing skills or my color choices might not meet someone else's standards. I have more confidence now, at least when it comes to baby quilts, since I recognize that most young mothers don't have much time, if any, to sew.

No, my biggest fear now is that my quilt will be held in *too* high esteem, that the parents will decide not to use it at all or to use it sparingly in an effort to preserve it. I made that mistake with the very first quilts that I made. Before my children were born I made them quilts. The first was embroidered, the second was machine-appliquéd, and the third was simply machine-pieced triangles. (Notice how they got easier as I had more toddlers running around.) All three were hand-quilted, however. I treasured them too much to even give them to my children! I put them away so early I don't even have pictures of my children with their quilts.

I think I wanted them to be in good shape when I passed them on to my future grandchildren. Almost everything that I had used as a child was passed on to nieces who were just three and four years younger than I was. As a result, I often didn't feel ready to give up my toys yet when I watched them go. All I have left are one doll-shaped rattle that was probably chewed on by some or all of my siblings and had lost too much paint for Mom to pass on, a green rabbit in similar condition, and an incomplete set of wooden bowling pins. Odd little treasures, to be sure.

I wanted my children to have several things that had been theirs when they were little to pass on to their own children, so I preserved the quilts. Not surprisingly, however, those baby quilts I carefully saved don't look familiar to my children. They have to take my word for which quilt was made for whom and that they really had slept with them. Their biggest value, their sentimental value, is limited because I protected them too much. I don't want other mothers and fathers to make the same mistake.

At a recent baby shower, I put a note in with the Four-Patch quilt I had made saying that machine washing and drying and even dragging the quilt on the floor will only make it softer. I was intending to express my hope that the quilt might become this child's "bankie" and didn't want his mother to discourage him from dragging it around. (And yes, we do know the baby is a boy.)

My daughter, Eden, gave a friend's little boy a quilt she had made that featured a large sailboat, a shore of pieced shell fabrics, and a blue sea and sky. She even hand-quilted it. She was overjoyed when the boy's mother told her he wanted to take it everywhere. If the quilt remains a favorite, in a year or so it will be a little faded and perhaps a little frayed at the edges, but oh, so soft, and pliable enough that little fingers can scrunch it. It might even be a little chewed.

I want that for the quilts I make. I want them to become the ratty old quilts that embarrass Moms and Dads. I want the young owners and their parents to feel something when, years from now, they find the quilt in an attic trunk. I don't want the quilt to remind them of me. I want the quilt to remind them of the child's babyhood.

I don't think the note I wrote was quite successful in expressing that wish. The puzzled, almost disgusted look on the young woman's face when she read it had me feeling as if my gift were being rejected. I was a little shocked at the embarrassed and hurt feeling it gave me, even though it didn't last. The mother-to-be seemed pleased enough by the quilt itself.

I puzzled over her expression for the rest of the party, thinking at first that perhaps my note didn't make sense since she read it before she saw the quilt. I finally concluded that my somewhat poetic wording had confused her. If she hadn't yet thought beyond an infant child, she might have interpreted my note to mean that I expected *her* to drag the quilt around on the floor to make it softer.

Dana

That moment of embarrassment, though, made me realize that I'm more vulnerable than I thought. I haven't completely outgrown self-absorption after all.

Buddha said, "If you knew the benefit of generosity, you would not let an opportunity go by without sharing." This practice of giving is called *dana* [DAH-nah], a Sanskrit word roughly meaning generosity or gift.

Marge Glasgow and her "attic angels" are a good example of dana giving. Marge began making stuffed angels to donate to her church's bazaar and other fundraisers. Her angels are stitched of tea-stained muslin and dressed and decorated with scraps of fabric, ribbon, lace, and old doilies. They have stuffed wings, yarn hair, and pantaloons. Their aprons are made from old embroidered dresser scarves and pillowcases.

Marge's daughter, Kim, a hospice nurse in Cincinnati, Ohio, mentioned that her terminally ill patients often talked about angels, so Marge sent her some for her patients. Kim reported back that the patients hold them and don't want to put them down. Often the patients give the angels names.

Marge is aware that some of the recipients will only enjoy the angels for a few months or even weeks, but if the angels bring the patient joy for even a short time, it is well worth the hours it takes to make one. She gets an occasional request for an angel, but if someone just wants one as a decoration, she declines. However, when an acquaintance told her about a teen-ager in Texas who was waiting for a kidney and heart transplant, she was happy to send an angel.

There's so much symbolism in angels, whether you believe in their existence or not. They connect us to a spiritual world beyond ourselves, a world that is on the mind of most of the recipients. They symbolize protection and care, making them more meaningful than mere stuffed dolls. The fact that they come as a loving gift, from someone who knows of your troubles, makes them more comforting. Marge has vowed that as long as her eyes and fingers hold out, she'll keep making them.

Another good example of dana giving are the gifts that are clearly specific for the individual receiving them. When Barbara Shunn, who is now senior branch office administrator at my local Edward Jones office, was a little girl, one of her cousins had to have surgery to correct a lazy eye. The cousins all knew that this child would have to wear an eye patch for awhile, which seemed like a really big deal to them. Grandma made the child a teddy bear, which in itself wasn't uncommon. She had made several. But this one had an eye patch so it could share the child's ordeal.

Not all acts of generosity are dana practice, though. Several things can get in the way. My reaction when I felt my gift wasn't appreciated illustrates one. When we are thinking of ourselves instead of the recipient, we aren't really being generous. Giving to show off or because we expect something in return is self-absorbed giving.

When we make a gift by hand, tailoring that gift especially for someone, our self-absorption usually fades. Our gift is unique, and we really don't expect a similar gift in return. If we spend our time while we're stitching thinking about the recipient, our mind must necessarily shift away from ourselves. My problem with the baby quilt came when I anticipated my handiwork being admired by the others at the shower. My thoughts had not turned away from myself as entirely as I had supposed.

Another thing that trips us up is attachment to the gift. A handmade gift can take many hours to complete. We're perhaps *more* vulnerable to attachment in that case than we would be to something that cost us only money. This was part of my problem with the quilts I made for my own babies.

A dear friend of mine, whom I would never characterize as anything but generous, found herself quite upset after making a full-sized quilt for a relative. When she visited the recipient some months later she found "her" quilt tossed over the back of a chair, being used as a throw. She felt, perhaps rightly, that this was too rough treatment for the quilting stitches and fabric to take for very long.

The telling note in her story was when she referred to it as *her* quilt. She had invested too much of her time to be able to relinquish the gift entirely. The experience, and the feelings it produced, had a negative effect on her desire to make any more quilts for unappreciative people. And, of course, it isn't always easy to tell in advance who is going to be appreciative.

Another friend has made quilts for all of her children. When she was visiting at one child's house, she found a quilt she had made being used to protect a chair from the dogs. She was a little more philosophical about it, though. She said she didn't mind about the quilt, it belonged to the recipient now, but she didn't think she'd make any more quilts for that child. I think she must have minded a little or she wouldn't have thought to tell me the story.

Though both of these friends had similar experiences upon seeing their handiwork in its new setting, the second had an easier time of it because she had relinquished ownership of the item. Even though the time it takes to hand-make a gift can increase our attachment to it, making a gift with a particular person in mind can help us relinquish it.

As I stitch away on the Bear's Paw baby quilts or a table runner for my daughter-in-law—or even when I stitch giant buttonholes in tablecloths so my younger son can run sound equipment wires through holes in his mobile D.J. table—I think about the person I'm sewing for. I try not to confine my imagination to a picture of them using the item I'm making. They might not. As hard as I might try, what I make could be wrong for that person (except for the disc jockey's tablecloths, which were made to order). It's entirely possible that what I make might only see the light of day at their next garage sale. I try to think about that *person*—the happiness they bring to me and others, and their particular talents and personality. I'm making my gift for *them*. The recipients do not exist to safeguard my handiwork for posterity or to boost my pride.

Gifts shouldn't have strings attached, though sometimes we can hardly help it. I remember one Christmas when my sister Sally, probably a teenager then, gave Nora and me each a new doll along with several extra outfits she had sewn. She had intentionally bought dolls that were a little smaller than the really horrible baby dolls Nora and I carried around. She was hoping to replace the worn-out ones.

Sometime back before my recollection, my sisters had tried to feed one of a pair of matching dolls through the tiny hole at its mouth. The small amount of applesauce that got inside rotted through one cheek. Nora and I had decided—and this I remember—to cut a hole in the other doll's cheek so they would still look alike. I remember this horrifying the rest of our family.

These two disfigured dolls were what Sally was hoping to replace. Her plan didn't work. Nora and I were willing to expand our doll family and accept these new dolls without giving up the old ones. Besides, we could squeeze our old dolls into a couple of the new dresses, much to Sally's frustration. We were sort of socialistic in our beliefs and it wouldn't have done for two dolls to have that much more than the rest.

The gifts were a great success with Nora and me, even though things didn't turn out the way Sally had wanted. She gave in (or gave up) fairly graciously, though.

Another time that our motive can interfere with true, unselfish giving is when we give out of a sense of tradition or obligation. I gave a quilt to a nephew's child because I'm very fond of that nephew. Another nephew had a child at about the same time, so I felt obliged to make a quilt for his child as well.

However, the act of giving itself can sometimes purify our motives. In giving this second nephew's baby a quilt, I had an opportunity to get to know the young mother. (At my age, they *all* seem extremely young.) I came away glad that I had bothered, but more than that, glad that this mother and child are part of my extended family.

This is perhaps the most important part of dana practice, the kindness toward the recipient that can develop when we overcome our own self-absorption and give up our attachment to something. Whether the gift is handcrafted, a monetary donation, our energy in the form of service, or even our wisdom when we share our knowledge in some way, it can be dana practice.

Assorted Attachments

One way of looking at the goal of Zen practice is as an attempt to become more deeply involved in life and at the same time less attached to it. I'm sure how we understand this idea changes with our circumstances and as we age. For me it's a reminder that life is short.

Some might see it as an excuse to have as much fun as possible—to go for the gusto, as the Schlitz beer commercial used to say. Put a little more gently, it may remind us to stop and smell the roses. In needlecraft language, it means to stop putting off those projects you've been wanting to try.

Another might see it as an admonishment to slow down, to stop working so hard to accumulate wealth or possessions that will be meaningless in the end. I wonder sometimes just what my children will do with all my accumulated fabric and yarn after I'm gone, not to mention my vast collection of embroidery hoops.

And what is "life" anyway? Is it what happens while we're making plans? Is it a composite of those changes that go on around us that are beyond our control? We all have lives, of course. What do you think of as the center of your life? Your job, your family, your religion, your social life, your hobbies, your dreams of something more?

Sometimes I think my life is pretty narrow, or maybe I'd just like it to be. I think I would be happy if I could stitch, write, and garden surrounded by my family and forget about everything else. Besides being impossible, this would be like living with blinders on. Life would be going on in my peripheral vision, and I wouldn't really be able to ignore it.

The other extreme would be to take all the world's problems to heart. Psychologists say that this isn't healthy, either. We can't solve them all, but there are places where we can lend a hand. The trick is to find what we can do, where we can apply our talents on behalf of someone else.

Most of us have heard of quilting bees, but neighbors used to have sewing bees as well. The Wyoming homesteader Elinor Pruitt Stewart described two in her letters. One she organized herself, not as a social gathering, which they always were to some extent, but to help out a particular family. On this occasion, she met a teenage girl who was living with her grandparents. The grandfather had arthritis in his legs and the grandmother in her hands. As a result, the young girl was doing all the work on the farm. The grandfather had tried to sew the girl a dress, but it had turned out rather badly.

Elinor suggested that a close friend of the old couple visit them and get some measurements and all the fabric the family had on hand. Other neighbors donated fabric as well. Elinor made underwear out of flour sacks, since that was what she had on hand. She did her sewing in advance of the gathering so she would be free to act as hostess for the party, as she called it. They made more clothes than the young girl had ever seen at one time.

The other sewing bee was more spur-of-the-moment. During a winter hunting trip into the mountains, Elinor and her friends encountered two women and their children living in an otherwise abandoned logging camp. Their husbands, they later learned, had gone into town, gotten drunk, and lost all the money that they were supposed to use to buy supplies. They were still in town trying to earn back the money.

Meanwhile, the families had given them up for dead and were becoming desperate. One had just given birth to another child, which made it difficult for them to leave the camp.

The men in Elinor's hunting party killed and dressed a deer for them and the women went home and sewed. There was no time to get to town for new fabric. Every discarded garment was made into something for one of the children. They sewed into the night until they couldn't keep their eyes open. The next morning, they returned to the logging camp with their gifts.

I'm afraid that in our modern world we don't think to do things like that. If I met someone who appeared to be in need, I wouldn't run home and sew for him or her. Because of all the thrift stores around, I probably wouldn't think of it as a primary need. I think, too, that most of us are more comfortable with faceless charity.

A few years back, the deacons of my church gathered supplies for school kits to be distributed by Church World Services. These were filled with school supplies, such as paper, pencils, scissors, and small boxes of crayons. We've done medical kits, too, but the school kits called for small book bags. The first year, Nancy Collins shared her pattern with me and we made eight bags. Each of the following four years, we got more donations of school supplies and were able to put together more kits, up to fourteen one year. The deacons moved on to other types of projects, but Nancy and I were wondering recently if it might be time to try the project again. Nancy says she's got some great book bag fabric saved. For me, part of the joy of making the school bags for the program was imagining many different children who might receive one of the kits.

This was different from the other times I had donated something I had made to a charity. Most of the time, I donate something that I've made and decided later I didn't need. The book bags were intended for a stranger from the beginning.

I made one baby quilt that I intended to donate to the church deacons from the very beginning. This was before so many of my nephews started having babies all at once. I had no immediate use for a baby quilt, but I wanted to try out a construction technique on something larger than a potholder but not unreasonably large. A baby quilt seemed the perfect size and it was something I knew the deacons would be able to give away.

What I wanted to do was see if I could piece a quilt directly onto the backing and batting. This is only going to work with a Log Cabin, Courthouse Steps, or other block pattern in which you start in the center and work outward. I had used the technique on a potholder before I decided to try the baby quilt.

The decision to donate it to the deacons to give away as a draw for donations was reinforced by the fact that most of the fabric I decided to use had been free. For a couple of months a few years ago, I worked in a gift shop. They sometimes used sale fabric purchased at a nearby fabric store as background for displays. Before I started working there, they had used a bright teddy bear print. My second or third day of work, I discovered all this fabric in the trash, too dusty to use again. I peeled off the double-sided tape, took it home, and washed it. Since I was making the quilt from salvaged fabric, it seemed especially appropriate to give it away.

It brought in some money for the deacons' chosen charity, so I was satisfied. Carman Davis, who won the quilt, said that she just wanted to donate to the cause and didn't have any immediate use for the quilt either, but she would give it away eventually. Several months later, a couple in our church announced that they were expecting their first child. Carman happily gave them the quilt and now it belongs to tiny little Phillip. It's come a long way from the sale table at the fabric store.

The whole experience was so much fun, I've decided to do it again this year. I'm trying out a layered heart pattern. I'll sew three different-sized hearts on top of each other onto each block, split the blocks into fourths, shuffle the pieces and sew different ones together to make whole hearts again. I'll make it the size of a throw, hoping it'll appeal to a wider range of donors than a baby quilt would. I can hardly wait to start going through my stash for red and pink heart fabric.

Grace-Filled Getting

The other side of the giving coin is receiving. This, too, is part of dana practice. For gift-giving to help us let go of selfishness and grow toward our best selves, there must be recipients for our gifts. Some of the time we are each going to play that role for someone else. Will our actions help or hinder the giver?

Most of us were probably taught that it's better to give than to receive. Our parents and others were trying to teach us to be unselfish. Unfortunately, these early lessons may make us feel guilty when we are given a gift, especially one that clearly took the giver some time and effort to make. "Oh, you shouldn't have!" we say and truly mean it.

Eden, the expert cross-stitcher, made me a beautiful angel picture for Christmas a few years ago. This piece had to have taken hours and hours of painstaking work. If I had received the same gift from someone else, I would have been more alarmed than grateful. What were her motives? I would wonder. How embarrassing that someone would spend that much time on something for me! What must I make her to restore the balance of power between us?

But since it was Eden, I could accept it more gracefully. I know she's got a Zen attitude toward her cross-stitch. The joy is in the doing, rather than in the having. She *must* give away some of her cross-stitch, as I must begin to give away more of my quilts. Otherwise we will have no excuse to continue our favorite hobbies and our homes will be too full of our handiwork for us to breathe.

I knew also that Eden's angel cross-stitch and other handmade gifts she's given her father and me are expressions of love. It's easy to accept these gifts with the same feeling.

But what about the occasions when it isn't so easy? You may feel that the gift is inappropriate, perhaps more than your relationship with that person really merits. If they've given you more than you gave them, you are embarrassed. If you've given them more, you might feel slighted. And if it looks like the giver is treating someone else better than you, you can easily feel angry. You may be disappointed with the gift, feeling that it reveals that the giver doesn't really know you as well as you think he or she should. You may be suspicious of the giver's motives, wondering what exactly they expect you to give them in return. Or you may even be insulted by the gift.

When I was a young mother with three kids between the ages of two and eight or so, my husband's grandmother offered to do my mending for me. She didn't make the offer directly but through her daughter Lucille, my mother-in-law. I don't really remember how she presented the offer to me. Lucille was never one to impose on anyone and may have let me know that taking my mending to her mother would have been an imposition. Or she may have encouraged me to do it, knowing that it would give her mother something different to do. Lucille has always been very proud of her mother's sewing skills and surely let me know that the mending would have been done skillfully.

What I do remember is turning her down. I was a bit insulted at the suggestion that I couldn't mend my own family's clothes. I also had been taught not to impose and would have been ashamed to take my mending to Grandma's house. I would have been admitting that I couldn't do everything—which, of course, I couldn't. Because of all these feelings that the offer produced, I was unable to accept the gift Joe's grandmother offered.

Now I truly wish I had. Not that my kids ran around in rags because I had no time to mend their clothes. It wouldn't have made a great deal of difference in my life and even less in my children's. But it would have made a difference in Grandma's.

I know now that she watched me with my little brood and remembered raising three daughters on the farm when nearly all household tasks were very labor intensive. She remembered how busy she had been and wanted to ease my burden. She thought of all the things I was doing and came up with a way she could help. She could use her special talent with sewing and save me a little time by doing the mending. It wouldn't have been difficult for her to find the time and it would have been a labor of love. I should have accepted the offer, if for no other reason than the excuse to visit her more often.

When we are offered gifts that make us hesitate, we need to remember that without recipients, there is no generosity in the world at all. Our acceptance, simply and lovingly, makes it possible for someone else to practice generosity, to develop dana giving.

If we can accept a gift without questioning the giver, we make possible a true communication of regard and intimacy between us and the giver. And if the giver's motives are not pure, our graceful acceptance and appreciation may help purify them.

Even with all the best motives in the world, gift-giving doesn't always go smoothly. Barbara Shunn's doll, Vicky, disappeared one autumn when Barbara was six. Vicky simply vanished from the face of the earth, or at least the small part of the earth that little Barbara was free to wander. Barbara searched everywhere. She even looked under the bathtub, which sat a few inches off the floor on clawlike feet. As Barbara remembers it, she tore the house apart, desperate to find Vicky.

Then Vicky reappeared. In Barbara's memory she had been gone a long time. On Christmas morning, the cause of her disappearance became clear, at least in retrospect. She had been kidnapped by Grandma so Grandma could make her some new clothes.

Remembering the fuss she made about her missing doll, Barbara imagines her mother calling her grandmother and urging her to take some measurements and get the doll back home.

Zen teaches us that joy comes from making other people happy and suffering comes from trying to make ourselves happy. If we can practice dana giving in our daily lives, always living generously, and accept the gifts of others joyfully, we are on the right path on our spiritual journey.

 Try This

Make a small gift for someone without waiting for a special occasion. Choose something especially for that person. If he or she is a young person just discovering the joys of reading, make a bookmark by embroidering on a wide piece of lace. Make a scarf that goes perfectly with her coat. If a close friend has a special hobby, make a simple tote bag decorated with appliqué or cross-stitch to illustrate the hobby. Stretch your imagination and perhaps your skills as well. Keep dana giving in perspective and expend enough energy that you have plenty of time to appreciate that person while you sew.

chapter six

A Stitch in Time

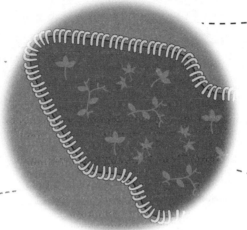

Tip: Mending

When patching a hole or tear, match the weight of the fabrics. If either the patch or the garment is heavier than the other, the lighter fabric will tear away from the stitches. Color matches are secondary. If threads have worked loose on an embroidered garment, never cut them. Use a tapestry needle or crochet hook to pull them to the underside of the fabric, tie them, and work the tails under other threads. You can mend a hole in knitted garments with yarn and a tapestry needle by pulling the yarn through the hole, mimicking the original stitches.

Wear and Tear

I had a favorite short outfit when I was little. I'm guessing I was
only three or four, though some people might say nobody actually remembers that far back. Whatever my age, I remember
the outfit. The top was essentially a halter top with strings to
tie behind the neck and back. Nora, of course, had one just like
it. I remember them being stripes on white, mine mainly yellow
and hers mainly green. I think I liked the short set because of
its unusual design and because it wasn't blue. It's also possible
that the outfit was simply new and only seemed special when
I was about to lose it.

I wore this favorite outfit outside to play. I think I was probably supposed to have changed out of it after a trip to town,
because I remember the deep regret and shame that I had been
wearing my favorite short set instead of something else. The
great catastrophe involved a barbed wire fence we had to crawl
under to get to a tree swing. Actually there was a gate, but it
was way out of the way. I misjudged the distance to the wire and
caught the seat of my pants on a barb and tore them.

I remember being terribly unhappy and Nora trying to
comfort me. Mom could mend them, she was sure, but if she
couldn't, Nora would never wear hers again either.

I'm sure that promise is why I remember the incident. It
seemed incredibly generous and startled me out of my self-pity
as much as it comforted me. I don't remember if Mom mended
the shorts or not. My guess is that she did, since she had already
had plenty of practice mending those L-shaped tears in her

little tomboys' clothes, but I couldn't wear the outfit to town anymore, which would have suited me fine. I could wear it more often for play.

People don't mend, alter, or remake things much any more. Historically, everything was mended or remade into something else. On the frontier, wherever that happened to be in the history of our country, new fabric was expensive or hard to come by. The unworn parts of sheets were remade into clothing. Men's worn-out shirts were cut down for children's clothing. Creative fabric reuse was also common practice during times of hardship, such as the Depression and the Civil War.

While I haven't run across any historical account of women using their curtains to make a dress as Scarlett O'Hara did in *Gone with the Wind*, I have read of Southern women cutting up their curtains to make quilts for their soldiers. In fact, during the war there were approximately twenty thousand soldiers' aid societies. In a sense, as Sarah Jane Full Hill wrote in her memoirs, "Every loyal household became a Soldier's Relief Society," turning anything that they could spare into bandages or bedding or knitted socks for the troops.

Even in less trying times, mending and reusing was taken for granted as a necessary household task until very recently. It has traditionally been women's work, but most women now are employed outside the home and evenings are filled with their children's school and sports activities, or their own. This leaves them little time to sew. Many women don't even own a sewing machine, which is often the easiest and neatest way to mend something. While people who like to sew are probably more likely to do the quick mending projects as they come up, most of them would rather be making something new. My mother's generation, however, would routinely take on even major mending jobs.

Nowadays most clothing is relatively inexpensive, and if a seam opens or a tear occurs, the garment can simply be discarded in favor of a new one. On the other hand, cheaper clothes are also more cheaply made, so you might discover an open seam in a brand new garment when you get it home. Knowing the basics of mending is still an excellent idea.

That said, I really don't like to mend things. I believe that torn jeans became a fashion statement because of a universal dislike of patching heavy denim. I'm hoping for holes, split seams, and missing buttons on everything else to become "in."

When I was a child, I would never have been allowed out of the house in torn jeans. Mom would have put a patch on my jeans before she washed them, because washing would cause the edges of the rip to fray, making it harder to mend. The patch would be big and ugly and feel funny, but the jeans would be acceptable to my parents. Children wearing torn jeans would have been considered neglected, and their mothers would have been considered lazy.

When my kids were in school, patched jeans were all right for play at home. I considered them safer, since a hole might catch on something, causing an active child to fall. However, at school, patched jeans made them look poor. Or so they said. Ripped jeans were cool. In fact, brand new jeans, in otherwise mint condition, with ripped knees were the coolest.

My theory is that children and teenagers were retrieving their torn jeans from the mending pile because they wanted to wear their old comfortable jeans ripped or not. (I might add, "before they outgrew them," but perhaps not every mother procrastinated as effectively as I did.) When one of the "cool" kids wore torn jeans, they became stylish. Soon kids were ripping holes in new jeans.

There were long stretches in my life when I let the mending pile up. I would attack the pile before a new sewing project to make room, or at least that was what I intended to do. I know there were times when the kids outgrew things that languished in a pile on the end of my ironing board. On the brighter side, there were also times when I mended and returned items that the owners had forgotten about, so they seemed like something new.

My sister Nora's kids call it the black hole effect. They would turn something over to their mom to be mended and never see it again. Nora tried to correct the problem by making a Lenten promise to sew something, mostly mending, every day during Lent. The notion was that she would catch up during those forty days, and she would develop a habit of mending often to stay on top of it. She says that sewing gives her a sense of accomplishment, even of virtue. Unfortunately, that isn't enough to make her enjoy it.

I love to sew. I love to see things take shape. I love the texture of the different fabrics, the disorderly rainbow of colors in my thread drawer, even the sound of my sewing machine whirring and clicking along. But I have trouble projecting all that joy onto the mending. It seems like a chore, not a pleasure. It's one more stupid thing, like paying bills, that I need to do before I can do what I want to do.

Nora and I both have memories of Mom mending in the evenings. We didn't have a television set until I was ten and Nora was eleven, so our memory of Mom mending includes a quiet living room. Mom would sometimes hum while she darned socks or resewed buttons. It's a peaceful, nostalgic memory for both of us. But it doesn't make us like to mend. Perhaps we both realize that there's a haze of fantasy surrounding the picture.

These days, my solution to the black hole effect is to try to mend things within a week of their being brought to my attention. If possible, I drop everything and do it at once, even if it means changing the thread on the sewing machine, a thirty-second task that I treat as if it were a monumental undertaking.

I'll admit that this new plan makes me feel virtuous, it impresses the family member who expected to wait—but mainly, it keeps from adding to the clutter in my sewing room, which has become the realm of a (usually) organized quilter with multiple ongoing projects. Besides, it gets a somewhat tedious task out of the way before it starts to weigh on me.

I also try to catch little tears and loose buttons on garments as they come through the laundry. You know the expression—"A stitch in time saves nine." I don't know how old I was before I realized that it referred to mending: mend a tiny hole with one stitch before it becomes a large hole requiring nine stitches. By carefully watching for things that need to be mended, I actually decrease the amount of time I spend mending. Always a worthy goal.

Normal Wear

I also try to be philosophical about mending. It's a little like cleaning up a spill on the kitchen counter or pulling a weed out of the flowerbed. It's part of life. It's karma.

It seems like the word karma has been overused some in the recent past. It's usually thought to mean fate. I remember John Lennon's song, "Instant Karma," in which he uses it to mean death.

Karma more accurately means God's law or the natural law of cause and effect, which does in fact include our own death. Our future is influenced by what we choose to do in the present. If I choose to ignore a tiny tear in a seam and continue wearing and washing the garment until the tear becomes a large hole, it doesn't make sense for me to curse fate because now I have to try to repair a seam whose edges are frayed. Unless I'm ignorant of the effect of washing on unfinished edges of cloth, I knew it was going to happen. I made my choice and have only myself to blame.

Zen teaches us that problems arise when we fail to see reality because we are projecting some ideal, some fantasy onto it. Nora's and my image of Mom pleasantly mending in the evenings may work against us. The actual task of stitching that button back on a shirt or darning a hole in a sock doesn't come close to our soft-lit, romanticized memory, so we set the task aside.

If we're honest, there's a bit of fantasy involved all the time when we're sewing. We imagine what our finished project will be like, for example. This is actually necessary for us to finish, or even to begin, a project. Something struck our imagination in the first place, making us want to create an item, making us want to see it through to the end. It's when our image of the completed project is unreasonable that we run into difficulties. We strive for that impossible ideal, but, at the first error, we give up. This can happen when we're mending, too. If we can't make the garment like new, we don't even want to try.

There is a Zen principle that no matter how hard we try, perfection cannot be accomplished by ourselves. Rather we must trust ourselves, with all our imperfections, to the reality. This is sort of the plunge we all take when we start a new project, including a particular piece of mending. We picture the outcome, but we leave it flexible enough to include the imperfections that will make it uniquely ours.

This may remind us of the catalog ads and clothing tags that explain away imperfections or "irregularities" by citing natural fibers and preparation techniques. Once we understand that these differences are part of the product's unique quality, we accept it and may even feel a certain pride in owning a garment that is unique. Unfortunately, we may have a harder time accepting such imperfections in our own handiwork.

Similarly, we sometimes harbor a subconscious fantasy that once-new clothes should stay new forever. We deny the normal wear and tear for as long as we can. Suddenly we realize that a garment is looking quite shabby and worn. With a shock, we become acutely aware of the passage of time, in ourselves as well as our clothes.

Loose Ends

With Zen, we attempt to be mindful of the reality of the moment, free from the distortions of fantasy. Two of the bad habits that often prevent us from seeing reality clearly are greed and ignorance.

If we want something, we can talk ourselves into just about anything, ignoring the bigger picture. My son Paul is in the Army National Guard. When he is on duty, he carries a little sewing kit with him that is designed especially for the soldier. It contains thread in colors that match his uniform and army-issue underwear. The Special Forces units have different kits to go with their specific uniforms, and so on. These types of things have been around since armies were first formed. In the 1800s they were called *housewives* or *caboodles*.

Paul tells me he's had to sew up a few split seams and tears, usually while he's still wearing the garment. (Barbed wire is often the culprit. I've had plenty of personal experience in that regard.) My son tells me that if a uniform reaches a certain level of fading or damage, it can be turned in for a new one. Often he has seen soldiers turn a small tear into a large one so their uniform will qualify for exchange, eliminating their need to mend it. They solve their immediate problem but contribute to the overall expense of the taxpayers, the very people the soldiers are committed to serve and protect.

Sometimes the end result of our ignorance of mending techniques or our greed for new clothes isn't all bad. If you frequent garage sales, you may have noticed garments for sale because of a minor defect that could easily be mended. The original owner may not know how to fix the problem or may be using the small defect as an excuse to buy something new. Someone who knows how to sew can reap the benefit.

A conversation with a volunteer at a thrift store that specializes in used clothing bears out my notion that a lot of people don't mend. They see lots of things coming in that need a little work. When they go through the clothes that are donated, everything that can't be slipped on a hanger ready to sell is separated out. These items are sent to a service that sorts the truly worn-out items from those that need a little work. The worn-out items are sent off to be recycled. They are eventually turned into such things as shredded bedding for pet cages or stuffing for plush animals. The fixable clothing goes to an organization that provides work for handicapped individuals. They mend the clothing, which is then sent primarily to Third World countries, but also to domestic charities.

Again, several people benefit from this process of use, reuse, and recycling. Donating your unwanted clothing, even if it's only because a seam popped open, is better than sending it to the landfill.

People don't always keep that in perspective, though. One of my sisters told me of a well-to-do woman who donated clothes to her church's garage sale but cut all the buttons off first. Greed kept her from seeing that the garments lost their value without the buttons. At my local thrift shop those clothes would have gone to the recycler, and perhaps that's what happened here as well. But not before one church volunteer pressed the button-hoarding individual about it. "They can find their own buttons," was her Marie Antoinette–style reply.

Zen teaches that a distortion of reality leads to dissatisfaction. It can affect others as well as ourselves, and the dissatisfaction can be felt immediately or down the road a ways. Was the donor of the clothing sans buttons going to be satisfied with her extra buttons? Did she really need them, or even use them? What are the odds that they are still in a button jar in her sewing room? Does she gain any satisfaction from her collection? When the soldiers who shirked their mending duties begin teaching their own children about responsibility, they may realize that they weren't as clever as they thought—or at least one hopes so. In the same way our romanticized image of Mom mending keeps Nora or me from being satisfied with the task as it really is.

The more we see things as they truly are, the more accepting we become and the more satisfied we feel. Saying, for example, that a particular dress makes me look fat is in a sense a distortion of reality. The truth is, the dress failed to make my overweight body look thin. The fault is my body, not the dress. I'm not suggesting that I should accept the fact that I'm overweight. Instead I need to accept the fact that my eating and exercise habits are to blame and change them, rather than searching for patterns and ready-made clothes that will magically make me look thin.

Incidentally, the volunteer at the thrift store said that there are also a surprising number of garments brought in that still have the tags on them. I have to wonder who found themselves that unsatisfied with a brand-new outfit, and why.

To Mend or Not to Mend

All this world view aside, when it comes right down to you and a torn garment, the decision to mend or not is likely to be a very personal one. How much do you like this garment? Is the fabric beginning to thin enough that another hole is likely to appear after just a few wears? What is the time consumption of mending compared to the cost of replacement? I am not going to darn a hole in a pair of socks I bought at six pairs for five dollars! Besides, I wore darned socks a lot as a child, and I believe that they can cause blisters.

A popped thread that opened a seam is the easiest thing to correct. The step that takes the longest is changing the thread on the sewing machine to match the garment, then changing it back for the work-in-progress—or at least that's how it feels.

When I used to set these things aside in a pile at the end of my ironing board, I had some fantasy that I would remember them when I finished one project and before I began another. I call this the thread transition plan. Mending would be done in groups by color, beginning with anything that could possibly be fixed with the same thread as the last project and ending with anything of a color similar to my next project. Notice that this requires a large accumulation of mending to work efficiently.

But I never wanted to postpone my next project while I mended! My distorted view of reality left even me unsatisfied if the garment happened to be my own. I'm sure my kids and husband were less than satisfied by the arrangement when the garments were theirs. Did you know that clothes will actually get dusty if they sit long enough?

Now, besides doing these little jobs right away, I try to see the bigger mending task as a challenge. Battery acid burns in my husband's new overalls (it never happens to old ones) or a rip in a favorite blouse or dress takes some creative thinking. Granted, starting something new is more fun. A new project holds so many possibilities; mending projects hold so few. Still, the problem can be taken care of neatly or carelessly. Neatly takes more effort, though sometimes not much more time.

In fact, one woman told me that one of her favorite tasks each spring and fall is going through her kids' clothes, sorting out what is in need of mending or too small. She could marvel at how much her children had grown and take great pleasure in altering one child's outgrown clothing so that it could be worn by the next. To her, if not to her children, it was like a shopping spree.

We had the same type of housecleaning when my children were home. As I remember it, it was more fun before they were old enough to take part. After a certain age, adding ruffles to boys' clothes did not make them wearable as far as my daughter was concerned.

Altered Reality

The extreme type of mending, in the problem-solving sense, is altering. This is sometimes a major undertaking, and until you've had some experience with it, it is fraught with difficulties—and sometimes even after. For example, a decade or so ago I had a dress of washable, wrinkled silk, the kind you were supposed to twist up and tie in a knot to dry. It was just a little too long so I decided to hem it up. How hard could it be?

I took the dress to my sewing room and discovered that the original hem wasn't particularly straight. This hadn't been noticeable when it was on, with all the folds obscuring the very bottom. The fact that it hadn't been noticeable should have been a hint that it didn't matter, and I should leave it alone.

But no. I decided I would straighten the bottom as I trimmed it to the appropriate length. This turned out to be impossible since the skirt consisted of several wedges sewn between flared panels. There was nothing to measure from except the uneven bottom. Eyeballing it turned out to be very deceptive.

If you've watched any slap-stick comedy you know how this turned out. By the time I trimmed and retrimmed the hemline, it was too short; not indecently short, just too short for that style. I donated it to the thrift shop, hoping someone even shorter than I am would get some good out of it. I didn't want to ask the volunteer I interviewed how many botched alteration projects were donated for fear the question would be the trigger that made her recognize me: "You're the one that brought in the pink dress with the screwed-up hemline."

I've had other catastrophes in my altering endeavors, but none I regretted quite as much as that dress. Usually by the time I attempt a makeover, the garment is useless as it is, so anything is going to be an improvement.

One of these learning experiences involved a dress I had ordered from a catalog. I loved the material, but the dress never seemed to fit right. After wearing it a couple of times, I decided to attempt some altering, thinking that it needed to be trimmed down a little, decreasing the bulk of the fabric where I already provided plenty of natural bulk.

I put the dress on inside out so I could pin up the seams. I quickly discovered that the sides didn't match and there were odd tucks and gathers that made no sense. I took out seams, thinking I could stitch it back together better than it was, only to find that the pieces hadn't been cut out well, there were jagged edges and some cutting slips were simply folded over or pulled into the seam.

I struggled with the dress, gave up, returned much later to struggle some more, then finally gave up entirely. The partially dismantled dress is now in my "exotic" fabric box. Some day it might become something "new."

Looking back, I realize that the dress was likely made in a sweat shop by someone who was required to work very quickly, perhaps even a child. At the time I bought the dress, I was ignorant of that possibility. It makes me wonder now how much our shopping habits affect the lives of people around the world.

You may have heard of the butterfly effect. The notion is that the flap of a butterfly's wings will affect the weather on the other side of the world. That's a little extreme to take literally, but it's the very essence of karma. The future, ours and others', is affected by our choices today, sometimes for good and sometimes for ill. Since we can't know all the implications of our actions, the best we can do is try to see past our illusions to reality and then act accordingly.

There's a bit of a paradox here. We are told to be mindful of the present, the here and now. At the same time, karma speaks to the effects, sometimes far-reaching effects, of our actions. The hope is that if we are mindful of the present, without the fog of fantasy obscuring the truth, we are more likely to act in the present in ways that produce positive karma for the future.

Ultimately all things decay. The clothes and other possessions that mean so much to us now will eventually go out of style, fade, or wear out completely. Nothing exists eternally, including ourselves.

Tradition says that Buddha's last words were: "All composite things decay. Work out your salvation with diligence."

 Try This

Take an honest look at the contents of your closet. Try to see each garment as it really is. Does it need a little mending or altering? Could a quick fix prevent a larger problem later? Is it something you actually wear? Or are you saving it for some fantasy future? Would someone else get more good out of it than you do?

Do a little research and find a charity in your area that takes used clothes. Clean out your closet, then make yourself something new.

chapter seven

A Coat of Many Colors

Tip: Delicate Fabrics

Delicate fabric will sometimes follow the needle into the hole in the needle plate. Use the straight stitch needle plate so the hole is smaller and try a finer needle. If these don't work, make a thread bunny. This is simply a folded piece of cloth you put under the presser foot just behind the fabric as you start stitching. It raises the back of the presser foot enough that it no longer pushes your fabric into the hole. To make one, fold a scrap of cloth in such a way that half of it is two layers thick and the other half is three or four. This gives you different thicknesses to use with different weight fabrics. Stitch around the thread bunny to keep it folded. Your finished bunny can be anywhere from as little as a couple of inches square to 5" or 6".

Records on Cloth

Embroidery and cross-stitch are uniquely suited for making decorative records of life's milestones. Needlecraft catalogs are full
of kits to commemorate weddings and births. Sometime in the
1980s, my sister Sally cross-stitched little pictures for Nora and
for me that had the name and birth dates of all of our children.
Nora has taken hers out of the frame and added another child.
Sally left plenty of room around the pictures for us to add our
grandchildren, too, if we want to. I treasure the little picture
because Sally made it, but also because of what it records.

When my older son, Jonathan, and his beloved Megan
decided to get married, Eden and I wanted to create something in
cloth to commemorate the event. None of the kits we had seen
really looked right to us so we decided to make our own. I made
up a cross-stitch pattern based on their wedding invitation and
Eden did the stitching. Jon and Megan were proud enough of it to
display it at the wedding on the table with the guest book.

On certain occasions such as these, our needlework becomes
transformed from ordinary cloth and thread to something more.
Because of what they symbolize, they take on a nearly sacred
significance that only increases with time.

Tiny Gowns

In one of her usual long letters, Wyoming homesteader Elinor Pruitt Stewart tells the touching story of a young woman

who found herself in more trouble than she could handle. Cora Jane fell in love with a man whom her parents didn't approve of. Before the man could convince her family that he was worthy of their daughter, he was shot and killed. A rather colorful neighbor woman, Mrs. O'Shaughnessy, who turns up in many of Elinor's letters, helped Cora Jane move into the house her love had been preparing for them.

Cora Jane was pregnant and decided that she would die when the baby was born. She wanted the baby to know that it was loved, however. Unable to convince Cora Jane to live for the baby, Mrs. O'Shaughnessy suggested that they make the little clothes with extra care. Though she is often described as rounding up cattle or hunting, Mrs. O'Shaughnessy was also an expert needleworker. The little outfit that was saved is described as "dainty enough for a fairy" and was treasured by the orphaned girl many years later.

Toward the end of the same letter, Elinor mentions that a dear little child had joined the angels. Elinor made a gown, helped make the casket, and arranged the funeral. It isn't until a letter dated two and a half years later that she identifies the baby to her friend: her own son Jamie. Her help with the casket had included sewing the padded lining. In the later letter, she described the sad pleasure of doing it all herself. She had been so sad at the time that she couldn't bear to tell even her dearest friend about it.

Perhaps Elinor chose to tell Cora Jane's story, which was almost twelve years in the past at the time she wrote of it, when she couldn't bear to really tell about her own baby's death, because both of these sad stories told of a mother's comfort in sewing for her baby and the symbolic meaning in the garments that were stitched. Just as she hoped that her own sewing would be a balm for her own loss, she observed that Cora Jane's orphaned baby girl was still cherishing the little outfit that was her last gift from her mother. I hope the orphan was able to preserve it and pass it on to a child of her own.

I have an infant gown that was my mother's. The dress itself is a fine woven cloth that was once white. The yoke and sleeves are a delicate crochet. The bottom is finished with a 2" scallop of crochet as well as an insert of crochet a little more than 1" wide a few inches higher up. Judging by the width of the gown at the underarms, I would guess that the dress would fit a child up to about three months of age. The gown is long enough that it would have draped like a blanket over a child's feet.

The dress is open for about 9" from the top in what I always took to be the back. You can see where a snap or some other fastener used to be just below the lace yoke. That appears to be the only fastener. The lace yoke, 2" of it, would not have stayed upright above the snap, which makes me wonder if the gown was possibly intended to open in the front with those lace points folding aside like a collar. Of course, little babies don't stay upright either, so it may not have mattered.

Family tradition holds that Mom wore the gown when she was baptized. A couple of things support this notion. The style of the dress seems consistent with christening gowns of the era (Mom was born in 1913). More convincing evidence to me, however, is the fact that it was saved, suggesting that there was symbolic meaning in the dress beyond the beautiful crochet.

It wasn't always protected, however. My older sisters remember being allowed to use it as a doll dress. The fabric is torn from the bottom of the opening to the top of the crocheted insert. My sisters confess to having fed their dolls, a favorite activity evidently, while the dolls were wearing the dress. This may have been when Mom took the dress back.

Nora and I, who came along after our older sisters had outgrown dolls, did not have access to the dress. I have a vague memory of seeing it at some point, probably in Mom's cedar chest where she stored the extra bed sheets. The chest was open on wash day when clean sheets were taken to the beds and again on ironing day so she could put the freshly washed and ironed sheets away. I recollect a notion that the cedar chest held more treasures than I was allowed to see. Probably, though, Mom just didn't want us messing up her carefully folded sheets.

I don't think Mom washed the little gown before she put it away. She may have been afraid that the crocheted lace wouldn't hold up to washing or concerned that the hard water on the farm would turn the dress yellow, as it did all other white articles after enough washings. However, the food smeared on the front did more damage than the water would have. Bacteria in the traces of protein ate tiny holes in the cloth under the stain.

There is also an ink stain about the size of a dime on the bottom round of lace, which I am at a loss to explain unless it was done during some haphazard storing while it was in my sisters' possession.

When Dad moved Mom into a rest home, a lot of her things were divided among her children, but Dad kept the dress. When he moved from the farm to an apartment in a retirement complex, more things were divided, but again he kept the dress. After many years at the apartment, he felt it was time to move into a rest home. Dad oversaw one more division of his property as everything except what would fit in a dresser or his desk was cleared out of the apartment. When he died a few months later, we had those last few things to go through. Among them was his wife's christening gown; he had kept it with him all those years.

It's a little odd that I, the one with the fewest memories of the dress, was the one who took it home. But I know about fabric. I recognized the lace as crocheted, and I could speak with some authority when I said it needed to be washed before it deteriorated any further. I don't remember that there was anyone else eager to have it. Ink stain, ancient food stain, rip, tiny holes, and an overall brownish color did not make it look attractive to anyone but me.

I took it home and washed it in a very weak bleach and soap solution, turning it a creamy white. The stains, except for the ink, are light, the holes tiny, and the rip is in what I'll accept as the back. All in all, it's a beautiful little dress.

Part of the beauty, of course, is the symbolism. We're certain that Mom wore the little dress. We know that Dad treasured it. It's now a sort of sacred relic, cherished for these reasons and for its age.

I wish I knew who crocheted the lace and cut and sewed the soft fabric. The seams in the fabric were done on a sewing machine. The seams in the lace are hand-sewn in a tiny hidden stitch. I believe the crocheting is handmade, but whether my grandmother or some other relative did the work or a professional did it, I'll probably never know.

I have two doilies that I remember being around the house when I was a child. They each have cloth centers surrounded by crocheted edging. The crocheting is done with much heavier cotton thread than the dress, but the crochet is fastened to the cloth in the same way, one showing considerably more skill than the other.

As with the dress, the doilies' crochet has held up better than the fabric. I would replace the centers if I thought I could do it without making a mess of the task. The crocheting was done directly into the cloth, rolling the edge of the cloth under in the process. Cutting the cloth away and sewing the crochet to a new center isn't going to look the same.

My theory is that my mother made the doilies and her mother made the dress. I'm basing this on the fact that the doilies bleached out a couple of shades closer to white than the dress, providing evidence, though not proof, that they are not quite as old. The content of the fabric might influence the color as much as the age would.

A more complete story would enhance the value of the dress, but I will treasure it for what I do know of its history and for the example of fine workmanship that it is.

Textile Treasures

Among the things my sisters and I went through after Dad moved to the rest home was a stationery box full of old fair ribbons. Among the ones that are dated, the oldest says 1929. Dad would have been seventeen. A great-niece and I were the only ones interested in the ribbons. We split them up, sharing ideas of how we might display them.

Because of their age and because of what I know of my father's life in the 1920s and 1930s, I treasure those faded old ribbons more than the brand new Best of Fair rosette I got this year for one of my quilts. I have decided to mount them individually and by twos and threes on plain muslin fabric. These squares, though they will be different sizes, will become quilt blocks, separated by different-width strips of feed-sack fabric. I don't have a great deal of the old feed-sack material, but I think I have enough to make this work. I'll back it with more muslin, quilt around the ribbons and possibly in between, and have a wall hanging.

If I do this, the wall hanging will be interesting, but not beautiful. A lot of the ribbons are in pretty bad shape, and I may not include them all. You will have to use your imagination to appreciate it.

Laurel Thatcher Ulrich, in her book *The Age of Homespun* (New York: Vintage Books, 2001), describes many antique textile treasures dating back to colonial days. For these bedspreads, table linens, and embroidered samplers to be preserved for more than 200 years, someone had to view them as worth preserving.

In most cases it wasn't the beauty or perfection of the piece itself, but rather the love and respect for the person who stitched and in many cases spun and wove them. The craftswoman would save her best work for special occasions, giving it an aura of reverence to offspring and saving it from excessive wear. In colonial times, and probably to a large extent today, household items like these were passed on to daughters. How the second-generation homemaker regarded her mother's work would be a huge factor in determining the fate of the piece. If the daughter respected it and passed it on, *along with its story*, to her own children, it would probably be preserved.

Still, there are a lot of things that can destroy cloth. Fire, mildew, and insects are all dangers, not to mention ignorance and neglect. It's karma again. Cloth will eventually crumble into dust. But if cloth weren't so vulnerable, we wouldn't be in such awe of a 200-year-old handwoven counterpane or a 150-year-old tablecloth with hand-tied netting lace or even a ninety-year-old christening gown.

I want to make a pilgrimage to Bayeux, France, to see the Bayeux Tapestry. It isn't technically a tapestry but rather a crewel embroidery work, 231' long by 20" high, depicting the 1066 invasion of England by William the Conqueror of Normandy. It is believed to have been designed and stitched within a generation or so of the events it celebrates.

The fact that the work has survived for more than 900 years is astounding to me. Reading about its close calls at the hands of unimpressed bureaucrats makes me wonder about the forces protecting it. According to Kay Staniland in *Medieval Craftsmen;*

(Toronto: University of Toronto Press, 1991), it was overlooked in 1792 when the Revolutionary Government of France ordered all artwork that depicted the "vanity" of the monarchy be destroyed. In 1794 the Art Commission for Bayeux prevented it from being cut into strips to decorate a float featuring, ironically, the Goddess of Reason. It was almost used as a wagon cover in about 1870 when a local contingent headed for service in the Franco-Prussian War. The Commissary of Police provided a substitute and the Bayeux Tapestry was saved. The town of Bayeux was also spared from bombings during World War II, which could easily have destroyed the Tapestry along with the town.

These incidents make me wonder, too, about the wonderful textile creations that have been destroyed. Of course, as exceptions, the surviving cloth items—not just the tapestries and great works of art but the everyday fabric items, too—become precious because of their rarity. Things that my grandparents used daily would seem so interesting to me today.

What did my grandmothers' aprons look like? I remember my mother's, but none of her mother's were saved, I'm sure, because they were all stained with use. I have the apron Joe's grandmother made for me, and it's similar in style to some my mother wore. I seldom wear aprons, though. Clothes are too easy to launder nowadays.

How did little boys dress when my grandfathers were children? Wouldn't it be fun to have one little suit of clothes? If you happen to have something that old, I imagine you're aware of its rarity. Most were passed on, worn out, and used as rags—or maybe some pieces were preserved in a quilt.

If I had a huge box of all the clothes I wore as a baby, its primary value would be as an example of what babies wore in the 1950s. Even so, I would love to have one little dress. It would seem sort of precious, even to me. Since neither my siblings nor I were baptized as babies, there was no particular experience to lend its sacredness to an outfit worn at the time.

I've saved both kinds for my kids, the huge box as well as the sacred items. I made the outfits that each was baptized in. I saved one frilly blanket apiece, all of which were gifts and not exactly practical, but perfect for that one Sunday service. I also saved the quilts I made them before they were born and the childhood companions of my two older children, soft blankets named Boo Bing and Pinky. But there are also at least two boxes of everyday baby clothes, some of which were lent to their cousins and later returned. Probably a third of the garments in the boxes are things that I made. Even if my children don't want to make their children wear them, I'm hoping they will want an item or two that their mother made for them.

Recently my husband Joe found a little pair of overalls in the bottom of one of his dresser drawers. It's one I made that all three of our children wore. The knees are a little threadbare, and the side seam is torn at the waist. They may have been getting a little tight for the last child before they were retired. I remember I sewed ruffled eyelet lace along the straps for our daughter and took it off again for her younger brother. I'm not sure how they came to be in Joe's dresser. He may have swiped them out of the "too small" pile that was destined for the attic. Or Joe might have been the one dressing Paul when he decided they were too tight and moved them to his dresser right then.

Whatever the case, he was pleased and touched to find them. He let me see them but wouldn't give them up. They aren't anything special, but what they represent in sentimental terms is significant. By the time the kids were wearing those overalls, they were able to toddle around after their daddy, "help" him build a tree house, hang a swing, or plant a garden. Because of the memories it invokes, the garment seems to hold those fleeting times within its weave.

When I was expecting my first child, my mother-in-law brought out a box of baby clothes. Joe has one younger brother, and after they had both outgrown things, Lucille stored them away. At around three, most kids start wearing out their clothes faster than they outgrow them, so that's as large as most of the clothes went. While putting the outgrown shirts and overalls away, she had hoped she might have more children, so she kept everything. By the time she knew otherwise, it was too sad for her to go through the box. When we went through it together, she was looking at those little boys' clothes for the first time since she had stored them away.

I'll never forget the mixture of joy, embarrassment, and nostalgia when she found a T-shirt with a large hole a couple of inches above the hem. Clearly one of the boys liked to chew on his shirt. "Why did I keep this?" she asked. She hugged the shirt to her breast, laughing with tears in her eyes. She held the shirt away, shook her head at the hole, then hugged it again. Maybe that one shirt that brought back memories so vividly was the one she most needed to save.

Again, it wasn't the shirt but what it represented that touched Lucille's heart. Ask anyone who is the curator of Grandma's quilt about his or her charge and you'll probably hear more about Grandma than about the quilt itself. Then ask someone to tell you about an antique quilt they've bought. See if there isn't a difference in the tone and body language, as well as the content of the answer. Value, even sacredness, isn't inherent in the fibers or the stitches but in the memory and meaning we place on the quilts, fair ribbons, garments, or stitched artwork we treasure.

Nothing Equals Everything

A famous Zen koan states that "Everything is sacred. Nothing is sacred." Things like this give Zen the reputation of being inexplicable. But really it's very simple. If we are all connected and separation between the subject and the object is only an illusion, we are all part of one interconnected life force, sometimes referred to as the mind of God. In that sense, everything is sacred. However, by definition, sacred means something set apart, something separate. Since there is no separation between anything and ourselves, nothing is sacred.

Sacredness comes from what we project onto the object, rather than anything inherently special about the object itself. What the object (christening gown, minister's robe or stole, ancient table linen, or whatever) symbolizes can make it seem sacred. A wedding dress is a perfect example. I made my own out of eyelet lace rather than the usual satin. The style is simple, sort of late-flower-child. It's almost ankle-length with an Empire waist and short puffed sleeves. The fact that it's simple doesn't reduce the symbolism. Neither does the fact that I made it myself actually increase it. It is the dress I wore when Joe and I got married. That's where it gets its meaning.

We think of wedding dresses as creations in white satin and lace, but this wasn't always true. According to Peter Lacey in his book *The Wedding* (New York: Madison Square Press, 1969), a great many of our wedding customs are a refinement of the Elizabethan English customs. Whether she wore silk or linen homespun, the bride's gown was the best the family could afford. While she wore white for innocence, the gown would also be decorated with ribbons tied by her attendants in love knots. The bride chose the color of ribbon depending on what she believed the color symbolized. Modern brides' choices for wedding colors are usually based on personal preference and current popularity of the colors in styles. Any symbolism in these colors is generally subconscious.

In ancient Rome, the bride wore a straight tunic. Her mother tied a wool belt around her waist in a "knot of Hercules" for her husband to untie later. During the procession to her new home, she was often followed by two women carrying a distaff and a spindle, tools for spinning thread. They were intended to symbolize her willingness to take on the duties of domestic life.

In thirteenth-century France, the bride herself might spin a little wool or flax during the ceremony. She wouldn't have worn white, though. Styles were colorful then. Multiple layers in many colors would have suited her. The groom would have been just as vividly dressed.

The white wedding gown began in Victorian England when white symbolized purity. Marriages were actually unions between two families. The bride represented a continuation of the groom's family and, from their point of view, must be pure.

Many of our modern wedding customs have their roots in a time when people believed in magic or good and evil spirits. Since marriage marks a major change in two persons' lives, it makes them particularly vulnerable. Attempts to scare away the evil spirits have evolved into gunfire during wedding celebrations in the Middle East and cans tied to car bumpers in Western societies.

In Medieval Egypt, the wedding couple might exchange clothes for the wedding procession from the bride's home to the church and back again to fool the evil spirits. A decoy couple, dressed nearly as fine as the bride and groom, was more common. The best man and maid of honor serve that purpose as well as being the primary helpers to the wedding couple.

The veil is an example of a custom that crossed many cultures and continues, in an abbreviated form, today. Christian, Jewish, Muslim, and Hindu brides all might wear veils, which were originally intended to protect the bride from the evil spirits. On the other hand, in Morocco and Ancient India the veil was intended to protect other people from the bride. She was believed to have the "evil eye" until she had been purified during the wedding ceremony.

Influenced by the Puritans, weddings in eighteenth-century England and America were often much simpler than they had been. The bride wore her best dress, often new for the ceremony, but not a one-day-only gown. The veil was discarded as well. The movement didn't last, at least not for most brides. Within a couple of generations, the big-production wedding was back in style, complete with elaborate costumes and usually some remnant of the veil.

But there have always been some unconventional wedding dresses. The Wyoming homesteader Elinor Pruitt Stewart made one of those. She had taken in young Gale for a few months while Gale's mother attempted to seal a marriage deal for Gale's prettier but spoiled twin sister. The mother claimed that Gale's presence was spooking the prospective groom. But actually it was Gale that the young man wanted. Gale's mother must have been too angry or disappointed to hold the wedding for her less-favored daughter, because it fell to the Stewarts to hold the wedding. Elinor sent her Scottish husband to town for fabric for the wedding dress. He returned with "the gayest plaid outside of Caledonia." The bride was a very practical girl and agreed to wear the unusual dress.

While I was making my own wedding dress, which was a little unconventional in its own right, I thought I might possibly wear it again. It was really just a warm-weather dress not unlike the then-current style. The symbolism of a wedding dress didn't actually soak in until after the fact.

Sometimes a garment's symbolism is immediately clear to everyone except the one doing the sewing. An example of this is the story of Joseph in the book of Genesis in the Bible. Joseph is the firstborn of Jacob's favorite wife. Jacob has many sons by his other wife, but he loves Joseph best. Jacob, wanting to do something special for his favorite, made him a special coat.

This coat is traditionally described as a coat of many colors. Quilters love this description because we picture a busy patch-work of fabrics in the coat. More recent translations describe it as "a long robe with sleeves" (Genesis 37:3, NRSV). Long sleeves would hamper a laborer, so they were a symbol of a more elevated or privileged position.

Whether it was the cut of the coat, the fabric used therein, or the simple fact that it was a father's gift to one son at the exclusion of the others, the symbolism was clear to his broth-ers: Joseph was loved more than they were. Joseph irritated his brothers even more by telling them that he had been dreaming about them all bowing down to him. It got to be more than the brothers could stand.

When Jacob sends Joseph, who is clearly not working, out to check on his brothers who are tending their father's flocks, the brothers see their chance to be rid of Joseph. They seize him and sell him to an Arab traveling with a caravan of trade goods headed for Egypt. They take his coat, dip it in goat's blood and return it to their father, saying that their poor little brother must have been devoured by wild animals.

The coat, which symbolized Joseph's superiority, becomes the means of covering their evil deed. Jacob would instantly rec-ognize the coat and, in his shock at the blood-covered symbol, look no further.

Joseph goes on to do well in Egypt and his brothers do eventually bow down to him, but the coat is the catalyst for all that follows. After the father's dana gift, it was karma.

A Monk's Robe

Zen tradition has a story of symbolic garments, in this case the robe of the master of a large Zen monastery. As old as it is, there may be more than one version of this story. I read it in *Zen Flesh Zen Bones,* compiled by Paul Reps and Nyogen Senzaki (Boston: Tuttle Publishing, 1957). Hui-neng was an illiterate peasant who, upon hearing a Buddhist speaking, sought out a Zen monastery so he could learn more. The master didn't think that he could have an illiterate monk, but, since he was impressed with Hui-neng's intelligence and understanding, he gave him a job at the monastery.

Several months later the master decided he should find a successor. He asked the monks to each write a short poem expressing his understanding. The best would become his successor. All the monks assumed that the oldest monk, Shen-hsiu, who had studied the longest, would win. His was the only poem posted. It expressed the idea that thoughts dirtied the mind, which needed to be clear to reflect reality. It read:

> The body is like a bodhi tree,
> And the mind a mirror bright,
> Carefully we wipe them every day
> And let no dust alight.

Hui-neng heard about the contest and asked a monk to read Shen-hsiu's poem. Then he asked the monk to write down one for him, which expressed the idea that there is no distinction between thought and the awareness that reflects them. It read:

The body is not a bodhi tree,
And there is no mirror bright.
Since everything is empty
Where can the dust alight?

In private the master presented his robe to Hui-neng, saying that he should be his successor. Assuming that Shen-hsiu would not like being passed over, Hui-neng took the robe and ran away. Three days later the angry monks caught up with him, led not by Shen-hsiu, who we can assume was wise enough not to be jealous, but by a monk named Ming, who was angry that the symbol of leadership had been removed from the monastery.

Hui-neng placed the robe on a rock and said, "The symbol of our faith shouldn't be taken by force."

Ming tried to take the robe but discovered he couldn't lift it. He turned to Hui-neng and requested, "Teach me."

"If you want to be taught, think not of good and evil. What is your original face, which you had even before you were born? If you find your true face, the secret is in you."

Suddenly everything fell into place for both Ming and Hui-neng and they were enlightened. I don't know that hearing these words would instantly change my life, but these two monks had spent years of study and meditation.

Anyway, the symbolic robe was returned to the monastery and Shen-hsiu eventually wore it. Hui-neng went into the mountains to meditate for a few years before becoming a teacher.

I am sort of amused by the magic element in the story. While they were preaching reality, the robe becomes a sort of King Arthur–style sword. Perhaps Ming knew he wasn't worthy of the robe and his mind prevented him from lifting it. Symbolism can be very powerful.

If you don't believe me, put on a policeman's uniform and see if it changes you. Don't discount the trouble you could get into for impersonating an officer. Trade that uniform for the collar, stole, or other trappings of a priest or other religious leader. Do you feel different?

The change is not in the garment itself, but in our expectations and associations with it. The same is true of Grandma's quilts or the little christening gown. We don't really want to see reality. The wear and age are easily visible to anyone who doesn't treasure it. But we look into these sacred relics and see their original faces. We want to preserve that for as long as possible.

I have plans for my mother's christening gown. I want to put it into a shadow box–type frame along with a picture of Mom when she was little. Unfortunately, I don't have a picture of her in the dress. In fact, the earliest picture I could find of her was taken when she was probably three or four years old.

My quandary is how to attach the dress into the frame without damaging it. It seems to me that sewing it in would serve the best. I could possibly sew it to interfacing-backed fabric and glue that fabric to the back of the frame. It would be difficult to get it to hang just so, though. Besides, the frame isn't long enough to have the dress hanging full length. I picture it tucked and draped in such a way as to hide the holes and show off the crocheted edge at the bottom.

I've thought of putting the dress on a little hanger and fastening the hanger to the top rather than the back of the frame. I'm a little worried that a metal hanger might stain the dress, but a plastic hanger wouldn't look appropriate for a 1913 gown. Wood would be best, although untreated wood will stain fabric, too. Finding a wooden hanger the right size is unlikely, but perhaps I can find a simple one I can cut down.

I'll keep meditating on the possibilities. In fact, I may seek the advice of a master who has studied and meditated on such things longer than I have, such as a professional museum curator. At some point a plan will become clear, and I'll have enough confidence to tackle the project—to lift the robe from the stone, so to speak.

 Try This

Spend a little time with a treasure from the past. Display a quilt you've kept stored away. Frame your grandmother's lace handkerchief. If you don't have anything like this, visit an antique store and see if you can find an embroidered tea towel or handkerchief that reminds you of something an older relative or close friend used to use. Take it home and hang it on your wall or turn it into a pillow. Try to see the object as it would have been when it was new. Consider the symbolism of your choice and your connection to the past.

chapter eight

Stitching for Dollars

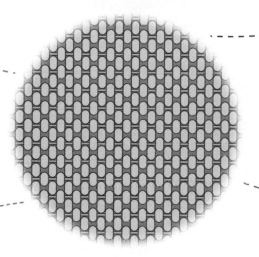

Tip: Stuffing

When you are stuffing a pillow or cloth toy with polyester fiberfill or cotton stuffing, pack the stuffing in firmly tight. Otherwise the stuffing will crush together and leave your project looking limp fairly quickly. One way to pack the stuffing is to use a wooden spoon. Use the handle end to pack the stuffing into the corners and the bowl to pack in between. Nothing on a wooden spoon is sharp enough to endanger your fabric or seams. If you are using foam rubber, cut it the same size as your pillow. The corners will crush down when you insert it into your pillow, preventing a boxy look. Embroidered faces and other embellishments are sometimes best added after the stuffing when the true dimensions are visible.

Crafts for Sale

Every once in a while someone will suggest that I sell my quilts or afghans or cross-stitch or in some other way turn my sewing "professional." I have several arguments against it, but I'm not sure that they are the real reasons.

Take selling my quilts, for instance. Depending on the location, handmade quilts sell for $200 to $400. This looks like wonderful money for doing what you want to do, and it is—until you break it down. The fabrics and supplies usually run between $60 and $100. Depending on the complexity of the quilt and especially on the density of the quilting, one quilt can take hundreds of hours to complete. The selling price then could amount to less than fifty cents an hour.

Logically, getting paid fifty cents an hour to do something you love is better than getting paid nothing to do the same thing. Emotionally, however, putting that small a value on my time actually cheapens my quilts and devalues my creativity. When I'm making anything for myself or as a gift, I can pretend that it's worth a million dollars.

Of course I could buy a quilting machine to cut back the time it takes to make a quilt. That would be a major investment, though, committing me to a large number of quilts to make it pay for itself as well as the other costs of making a quilt. At the same time, it might lower the sale value of the quilt.

Once, I actually did some custom sewing for money. When I was a junior or senior in high school, a classmate hired me to shorten a lined trench coat. I don't know if her mother had refused to shorten it or if my friend didn't trust her mother to do a good job. Perhaps my friend was afraid of the black-hole effect of the mending pile. At any rate, she hired me to do the altering for maybe ten dollars.

Her mother wasn't too happy when she found out about the arrangement and told my friend to get the coat back. By then, I had already done the work. I took out seams so I could hem the lining separately, the way it had been originally, and put it all back together again. As I remember it, it looked pretty professional when I was done. My friend was happy, and I think her mother was pleasantly surprised. At least that's what my friend said.

It was at about that time that my home economics teacher wrote "I would let you sew for me" on a grade sheet for a plaid pleated skirt I'd made. I took that as high praise. Actually, for a sewing instructor, who was not particularly lavish with her praise, to say this to a student seems even more exceptional to me now than it did then. At that point, I think I would have taken on about anything. If someone had suggested I could find a job at a clothing store altering or otherwise sewing professionally, I probably would have tried it. However, no one was going to hire a teenager to sew except another teenager, so I didn't sew professionally again.

Sometimes one thing can lead to another and you end up with a business you hadn't planned on. It began for Rodene Brooks when she made the bride's and attendants' dresses for one of her daughters' 1975 wedding. She had been sewing since she was five or six and had made her own wedding dress in 1954. Then her two sons got married and she made all of the dresses for the wedding party for both weddings. Then the sister of one of her daughters-in-law asked her to make the gowns for her wedding, too. From there it just escalated. Counting mother-of-the-bride and -groom dresses, she averaged fifty to seventy-five dresses a year for several years. The hardest part, she said, was trying to make attendants' dresses look alike when there was a great deal of difference in the sizes. When Rodene turned sixty-five, she decided to quit. At first she was going to say no to all requests, but she can't say no to her grandchildren.

Right Choices

The late Joseph Campbell, author of many books on the power of myths and a sort of inadvertent guru to free thinkers, believed that you should "follow your bliss." You should find some way to make a living doing what you love to do or, at the very least, find a way to make a living that allows you time to do what you love to do.

This is wonderful advice, but I think that turning a hobby into a business changes the nature of the activity. To me, working on needlecrafts is therapy. I find it absorbing and relaxing. It's also one of the few areas of my life where I feel I have control. I usually have several projects going and can choose which one I want to work on. If the project is a gift or a holiday decoration, I feel a sense of urgency to get it done, but most of the time

I can work at a comfortable, enjoyable pace for whatever length of time I've managed to carve out for stitching.

That would all change if I were sewing professionally. I would have to produce much more and do it more quickly to meet customers' expectations. Right now, I don't think I'd be particularly interested in even an occasional custom job because it would mean setting aside all of my other projects to do it.

Also, I am put off by the business side of sewing professionally. But then, I'm a little put off by the business side of writing, too. I solve a lot of that by having an agent. (Thanks, Mary Sue.) Writing and stitching mean different things to me, even though they are both creative and seem to steal time from each other. I don't want to write as a hobby any more than I want to sew professionally.

The whole point of Zen is to understand your whole mind. The more clearly you understand yourself, the less likely you are to jump into enterprises that aren't right for you. Remember the eight keys to happiness listed in Chapter 2? Right livelihood is one of them. How we earn our living impacts every other aspect of our lives.

Meditate on the aspects of your life that need to be in balance. Work and play. Mental activities and physical activities. Giving to others and receiving or saving for yourself. Are they in balance? How would that balance change if you were hand-stitching or sewing professionally? It might be that things would balance better for you, if you could find a way to make it work. Only you would know.

Jane's Story

About twenty years ago, Jane Snavely, the neighbor who, as a child, sat under her grandmother's quilt frame and pushed the needle back through for her, turned her sewing into a small business. She began by sewing quilted pillows and selling them at craft shows. Later she expanded into stuffed rabbits, cats, and bears. More recently she has been making custom curtains and draperies for two independent interior decorators.

The business side of crafts sales can be a little frustrating, she says. She has to have a sales tax number and be aware of the sales tax rate at the locations of the different shows. The people in charge of the shows are helpful, however, and often have their own tax number that vendors can use during the show if they don't have their own.

She has also put some of her crafts in area stores, but the shipping costs eat up her profit if she tries to place them very far away. And she never knows what will sell.

Among her quilted pillows one year was one in shades of peach that had turned out to be particularly beautiful. At her next craft show she displayed it prominently, using it to attract people to her booth. It worked great. A lot of people commented on that particular pillow, but no one bought it, and she had to take it home again.

On another occasion she was boxing up her stuffed animals to take to a show when she noticed that a few of them were pretty badly stained. She had made them out of an old quilt, and while she had tried to avoid the worst places on the quilt, she hadn't avoided the stains entirely. She debated on whether to even take them or not. She had room in her box so she tossed them in. They were the first to sell. They had character, the buyers said.

While she could buy her supplies in large quantities to save money, she could never charge enough to come close to earning minimum wage for her time. That didn't bother her particularly because much of the work was done while she watched TV, turning otherwise wasted time into something productive.

I have the same philosophy with my handwork, at least until I try to put a price on the item. Somehow I'd still want to be paid for all that time.

Jane's primary motive for turning her love for sewing into a profession has been to bring in some income yet still be home on the farm. Sewing at home gives her a more flexible schedule than any job in town could offer. What her husband Armand can do with one arm and a hook is amazing, but occasionally something comes up for which he needs two hands, and Jane likes to be available to help.

Moving on to custom curtains has saved her the time involved in attending the craft shows and otherwise trying to market her sewing. Although it's a little difficult sometimes to guess how long a particular project is going to take, once she's turned in her bid, she knows what she's going to be paid for it before she begins to sew. And she doesn't have to wonder whether or not it will sell.

She says it's harder on the nerves than sewing for herself, even with a locked-in customer. Just knowing that the fabrics cost as much as $100 a yard makes her tense and, according to her husband, a little hard to live with sometimes.

There are also challenges when she goes along to help hang the curtains, such as windows that go around corners or are positioned along curved walls. She's had to help hang curtains from the ceiling and has even encountered windows that weren't quite parallel to the ceiling or floor. Once when she was helping to hang drapes across a thirteen-foot span of windows, they discovered that there was no vertical stud above the windows in that entire span, giving them nothing to anchor a center rod support to.

Still, she has seen the inside of several interesting homes and has been able to maintain an income while remaining at home.

Just Us

Suzy Tuggle and Susan Retter started a small business turned cottage industry that eventually employed up to forty women doing piecework or other crafts out of their own homes. It began with a crafts club and Noel Nostalgia, a little shop the club operated in Concordia, Kansas, at Christmas time to sell their crafts.

Suzy and Susan partnered on some tea-stained dolls and then some Dirty Little Rabbits. Suzy has a degree in education with an emphasis on art and was the middle school art teacher for all three of my children. Susan has a degree in clothing and retail and knows how to sew. Suzy would get the ideas, Susan would make up a prototype, and then they would modify it together. The little stuffed, tea-stained rabbits got a lot of attention at the shop, and someone suggested that they see if Goose Crossings, a gift shop in nearby Belleville, might be interested in selling them.

Suzy and Susan packed up what they had and took them up to the shop where the owner bought everything. She was the one who put them in touch with a sales rep in Kansas City. The rep advised them to expand the Dirty Little Rabbits line.

Back home, the two women decided that if this were going to become a business they would need some capital. While they both got encouragement from their husbands, the women wanted the business to be independent of them financially. They went to the bank for a loan. The loan officer was incredulous. "How many rabbits are you intending to raise?" From the banker's point of view, the fact that both women thought of rabbits as dirty little creatures didn't bode well for them trying to raise them.

Once that misconception was straightened out, Just Us was in business. They started in Susan's basement then moved to Suzy's, which was larger. Eventually they rented a building downtown. They hired a couple they met at a market to represent them to sales reps. Dirty Little Rabbits were soon in stores all across the country. One of Suzy's biggest treats was opening a wallpaper book and seeing a pair of their rabbits used as a prop to show off one of the selections.

Meanwhile, they had expanded into a clothing line, beginning with appliquéd sweatshirts that were so popular other vendors complained about crowds blocking the aisles when they took them to craft shows. They found a source for some wonderful all-cotton jersey that didn't stretch out of shape, shrink, or pill. They started a clothing line they called Just Jersey with very basic skirts, tees, and pants in several different colors.

About the time they were becoming dissatisfied with the people representing them to sales reps, Just Us was named "The Women-Owned Business of the Year for the State of Kansas." The award made it possible for them to get their own sales reps.

This created more bookkeeping but also gave them more control. By this time nearly all of the sewing was hired out, as was the work on their line of dried flower arrangements. Suzy and Susan were quality control, making sure the sewing was up to their own standards. If they didn't want it in their homes, they didn't want to sell it. Of course, they were also buying all the supplies, from the giant boxes of fabric and stuffing, which were delivered to Suzy's quiet residential neighborhood in a semi, to perfectly matching threads and the little washing-instruction labels.

The Dirty Little Rabbits had a ten-year run. What Suzy and Susan were seeing at market led them to believe that the tea-stained country look was on its way out. They decided to discontinue the line before they had a drop in sales. They continued with the dried arrangements and the clothing for another five years. When they were no longer able to get the superior jersey fabric they loved, they dissolved the business. By then, their life situations had changed and they were ready to move on anyway.

Both women have good memories of the whole experience. They say they would do it again. In fact, my conversation with them made them both miss parts of it so much that I wouldn't be completely surprised to hear they were collaborating on some new item, something timely but uniquely theirs.

By the way, they copyrighted Dirty Little Rabbits. The process took longer than you would imagine and did them very little good. Anyone can still take the idea, change the slightest thing, and sell it as their own. They can't put "Dirty Little Rabbits" on the label, though. If you have one with that name stamped in ink on its bottom, you have an original.

Just Us worked because of the talents and personalities of the two women involved. Suzy had the ideas and Susan had the business sense, although I don't think the lines were drawn quite that clearly. They worked together on every aspect of the business and were able to laugh over their mistakes.

Susan's sewing skills made it possible for Suzy's ideas to see the light of day, but it wasn't long before all the sewing, except prototypes of new patterns, was done by others. Just Us allowed many local women to sew professionally out of their homes. Since these women were paid by the piece, they could do as little or as much as they wanted, working at their own pace on their own schedule.

Suzy and Susan even lost their housekeeper to the lure of sewing at home. Janice Brownell was cleaning several homes including Suzy's and Susan's. She was very interested in what Just Us was doing and asked to sew for them. It wasn't long before she was sewing enough that she decided to quit cleaning houses. Sewing was more fun than cleaning, she says, and she could do it at home.

Suzy and Susan were better prepared for the business aspect of turning professional than most of us, certainly more than I would be. I would be happier as one of the employees, stitching away in my spare time, turning in flat little rabbit bodies for someone else to stuff or sewing together skirts and tops. I might tire of it soon, though, longing to put my own creative touch to whatever I was making. Although I'll sew thirty-five identical quilt blocks together without being tempted to "get creative" with the thirty-sixth one, I rarely have any interest in making a second quilt of the same pattern.

The Factory Factor

It seems to me that the ultimate in tedious sewing would have to be sewing in a factory. Our first thought might be sweatshops in developing countries, but even a clothing factory in the United States doesn't sound inviting to me. To get an idea of what it might be like, I called an acquaintance who used to work for Scott Specialty, a local manufacturer of medical support apparatus such as knee or wrist braces and arm slings.

What was the first thing my friend (I will call her Ann) wanted to share with me? The wonderful way her mind could wander as she sewed at work. She could think about all kinds of things, even replay a musical concert she had heard the previous evening. One time she felt a smile come to her face. She doesn't know what exactly she had been thinking of but she remembers the feeling of complete peace.

At this, and probably most similar factories, the workers aren't supposed to talk. They are supposed to try to fill a quota, and talking will slow them down as well as possibly creating a distraction that could impact the quality of their work, not to mention endanger their fingers. This meant that there were no interruptions to the concert in her mind. At lunch and break times she got acquainted with her fellow workers.

Ann had done some sewing when she was young but wasn't really doing much home sewing when she took the job. In fact, she didn't apply for the job because of the sewing. The job happened to open up when she was unhappy with conditions at the laundry where she was working. The factory was air-conditioned, clean, and comfortable.

Because she wasn't doing much sewing at home, sewing all day at the job didn't really change the way she felt about sewing. She's trying her first quilt now, she says, so clearly the factory work didn't ruin sewing for her forever. It was different than sewing at home, though. The pace was faster because of the quota, and the projects she was sewing, as well as the materials she used, made it unlike any home sewing she would have done. In fact, the company didn't care whether she had sewn before or not because she needed to learn their machines and their products.

Ann worked there for three years, then changed jobs in favor of one with the school district that would allow her to be home during the summer. During the seven years she's been gone, she's heard from others who still work there about the inevitable machine and product changes. She hopes it's still the pleasant place she remembers and expressed a wish that all sewing factories would be such nice places to work.

Surprised? I was.

I was curious enough, in fact, that I called Scott Specialties and was referred to Linda Ashton, the vice-president of material management and a daughter of the founder of the business. She's also the newsletter editor for the quilting guild I joined last winter. Small, interconnected world.

She agreed to let me visit the factory, or more accurately, the largest of the three factories. Her father, Wilson Scott, started the business in 1958. Velcro was a new product then, and he saw a possibility of using it to fasten rib belts that were all being made with ties at that time, ties that were often very awkward for the wearer. His idea proved to be a success and he gradually expanded to more and more products, which today total around 600.

They began as a cottage industry like Just Us but now have between 170 and 200 employees in the three factories. The employees are probably 90 percent women, a great many of them farm wives. Many of the workers have been with them for twenty-five and even thirty years. They rotate jobs often so no one is stuck making the same thing for very long. Many, Linda told me, still do a lot of home sewing.

I mentioned that Ann had commented on the comfortable and clean working conditions. Linda said that because of the competitiveness of the business, she's never been able to tour another factory. She can't say for sure what other factory conditions are, but when they bought a facility in Ohio that was producing a similar product, they were all shocked at how dirty it was.

We began our tour in her office then moved through the factory. We made a brief stop at a conference room where new products and changes in existing ones are discussed. They get a lot of feedback from their customers. In fact, a physical therapist had been in the day before discussing some of the products.

On the factory floor—and yes, it is cleaner than my sewing room—I noticed several people with headphones. I thought they were perhaps hearing protectors, though it didn't seem that noisy at the time. No, it turned out that these people were listening to music or books on tape. A lot of the women listen to romances, and when the story gets exciting or steamy they sew faster. Linda said she warns them to be careful.

Scott Specialties tries to be a good neighbor as well as a good employer. They recycle everything possible. The scraps from foam products are sent to the packing department to cushion shipped items. Returned items are donated to AmeriCares. They buy their materials from domestic manufacturers as much as possible, but it's becoming more and more difficult to find fabric made in the United States.

In 1993 when unusual rainfall produced a great deal of flooding, they made sandbags. At the time they had a large quantity of parachute material printed with Muppet Babies that had been purchased to make pediatric arm slings. The distributor they were making them for had gone out of business and they were stuck with all this cute but tough material. It had been stored away for quite awhile, but someone remembered it. They donated it and their machines to volunteer employees who wanted to come in after hours and make the sandbags. They even made some in the production line. I wish I had a picture of the Muppet Babies sandbags piled along a rising creek.

I came away from the tour seconding Ann's wish that all sewing factories would be run like Scott Specialties.

Historical Perspective

The first textile factories in the United States began operation about 1830 in New England. Prior to that time, household fabric was either homespun or imported from England. During the years immediately preceding the Revolution, home spinning and weaving were considered patriotic. When the factories opened, there was a shift in patriotic sentiment. Now the machine age was going to build the new nation.

The people doing the actual spinning and weaving were essentially the same, however. Young women, from early adolescence until they were married, had done much of the actual work when the tasks were done at home. Most continued to spin and weave after they were married, but they had other responsibilities then. With the opening of the factories, young women made up nearly all of the work force. They would work for a few years to set aside some money or lift their parents' burden and quit once they married.

With more factory-produced fabric available, some older folks lamented the fact that women would now be idle, their spinning wheels and looms collecting dust. Women were still sewing, however. The truth was, with more available fabric, clothing expectations changed. People were no longer content to own only two sets of clothes. Standards of cleanliness were changing as well. It became popular for people to bathe as often as once a week, and they expected their clothes to be washed just as often. There was now much more sewing and washing to be done in every household. It's a good thing that Elias Howe invented a sewing machine at about that time to help with all that additional sewing.

In urban areas, before ready-made clothes became available in the 1840s, people relied on tailors and seamstresses to do much of this sewing. They would generally buy the fabric at a dry goods store and take it to the tailor or seamstress to be constructed. The prices charged for this sewing seem ridiculously low to us today, but only the middle and upper classes could afford the work. *Everyday Life in the 1800s,* by Marc McCutcheon (Cincinnati, Ohio: Writer's Digest Books, 1993), lists the bills of one itinerate tailor who worked in Connecticut between 1818 and 1820. He made two cotton shirts for sixty cents and a coat for $1.50.

The actual craft of spinning thread and yarn and weaving cloth lost some of its charm. The women who worked in the factory didn't take quite the pride in their accomplishments that their foremothers had. They didn't keep ledgers listing the spools and skeins and yards of work accomplished. The pace of their work had to match the speed of the machines rather than the pace of their own creativity. Still, few of them seemed to mind. They were being paid a steady, though meager, wage.

From the beginning of the Industrial Revolution in the late 1700s, more and more clothes were factory made. About seventy years later, another sort of revolution was quietly born on the West Coast: the invention of nearly everyone's favorite garment, jeans. Levi Strauss and his brothers were dry-good peddlers. When news of the shortages in the booming gold towns reached them on the other side of the continent, they loaded their supplies on a ship and sailed around Cape Horn. Unfortunately, by the time they arrived in San Francisco in 1853, the rush had peaked and begun to decline. Nobody needed more tents and Levi couldn't sell his brown canvas. What the miners needed was good tough pants.

According to an article by Ivy Darrow in the August 1994 issue of *Wild West*, Levi took his canvas to a tailor. The first Levi's were patterned after Italian sailors' comfortable trousers, which were called "genes" because their usual fabric came from Genoa, Italy. Even though these pants were made from canvas rather than genes, the name stuck and eventually became spelled "jeans." Levi didn't like the name and it wasn't until after his death that the company began using it in their advertising. Levi called them waist-high overalls.

This is a great story, but there are references to blue jeans or Kentucky jeans in magazines predating Levi's move to San Francisco. Perhaps Levi felt that his product was superior to the earlier Kentucky version and he didn't want it to carry the same name.

At any rate, Levi traveled to the outlying mining camps and incorporated the miner's requests—back pockets, reinforced seams, and belt loops—into his pants. In 1860 he switched from brown canvas to indigo denim. By 1890 there were 450 employees in his factory. By 1990 Levi Strauss and Company was the world's largest clothing manufacturer. Long before that, nearly every person in America owned at least one pair of jeans, and many of us would happily live in them. Whether they are Levi brand or not, they are part of Levi Strauss's legacy.

Levi Strauss not only changed the way we dress, he had an effect on the clothing industry as well. When he began using rivets to reinforce the pockets of his pants, he began producing an item that no one could completely copy at home. This added a bit more energy behind the move from home to factory production. The industry has continued to change. Now more and more manufacturing is being moved offshore. Cheap labor is the primary reason, of course, but we need to be wary of other laws that encourage industry to leave. I'm not afraid of a global economy as long as whole groups of people aren't exploited in the process. We're all one, according to the Zen masters.

It's a safe bet that sewing and the clothing industry will continue to change in one way or another. Spinning, which used to be practiced in nearly every home is almost a lost art. Homespun yarn and thread would be far too time-consuming compared to machine spun, and it isn't economical unless you're raising your own raw materials. Personally, if I had sheep to care for or a field of cotton to tend, I'd have even less time to spin. Weaving, while not forgotten, is definitely a specialty art. The weavers I know are making art more than fabric. The expense, not to mention the space requirements, of a loom keep many of us who might otherwise be interested from pursuing weaving as a hobby. Sewing may become just as unusual some day in the future. But at present, it's a hobby that seems to be seeing a revival. You might even find yourself one of those who goes pro, one way or another.

 Try This

If you don't want to sew or knit professionally, but want to make more than you really need to, sew or knit for charity. Afterschool projects might need tote bags. Contact your local school district and ask. Charity organizations might be looking for things to raffle off. Hand-stitched or knitted items are especially appreciated. Your local law enforcement agency probably has a policy of keeping stuffed toys or blankets in the patrol cars for children during traumatic incidents, such as car accidents or the arrest of a parent. Project Linus provides blankets for hospitals to give to children, especially those who come in for extended stays. If you can't find these or similar good causes locally, consider working to get one started.

chapter nine

Sat 'n Stitched

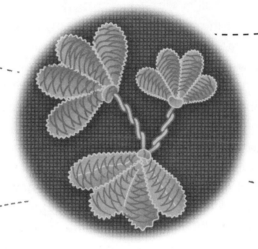

Tip: Needlework Backs

Try to keep the underside of your needlework as flat and neat as the front. It will, of course, have threads going in odd directions and not look like the front, but avoid knots and loose ends. Knots create a bump that may be visible on the front. Tuck the ends under the back of the stitches instead. If you skip from one area to another, tuck the loop under stitches in between or catch the loop under later as you fill in. If the distance is much more than an inch, you should stop and restart rather than jump across, especially if your thread is dark enough to show through your fabric.

Pick-up Stitches

When I was a teenager trying to get my knitting projects finished in time for the fair, I discovered that my best time to knit was in the evenings. I was not at all willing to give up television to finish my projects, so I learned to knit in relatively low light, by feel as much as by sight. I also discovered that I could get out of helping with the dishes if I picked up my knitting right after dinner, but that's a little beside my point. After I finished those first projects, I noticed that I missed the activity when I watched television empty-handed.

Now I find that I can hardly watch television without some kind of handwork. My family has nearly given up objecting to the light (not everything can be done by feel) because my fidgeting is even more distracting.

This isn't uncommon. Most avid stitchers that I know do most, if not all, of their work in front of the television in the evenings. An article in the September 18, 2004, issue of the *Quincy Herald-Whig* tells about a needlepointer whose husband loved to watch sports on television and wanted her to join him. Dorothy Grant found the games boring. "You could go downtown and get the groceries between football plays," she said. However, she liked to needlepoint and spent the hours stitching. She's gotten so good at it that three of her works are at the Embroideries Guild National Gallery in Louisville, Kentucky. The games her husband watched became her excuse to stitch, even though it may not have started out that way. Her husband is gone now, but she continues to needlepoint, though she doesn't watch sports on television anymore.

I don't think our choice to stitch away in the evening is exclusively a way to make television viewing comfortable. Most of the time our families don't care if we're sharing their shows with them or not, though sometimes we want to be there just to be near our families. Clearly, we can find something else to do if we aren't interested in the show that everyone else is watching. I think stitching in the evening helps us wind down from the day.

By evening most of us have been busy, perhaps a little too busy, all day. Our physical energy has ebbed, but our brains are still in "hurry" mode. We might even have trouble concentrating on the television if we didn't have our needlecraft to burn up the last of that tension. I wonder, if we taught our husbands to knit or embroider, would they stop flipping the channels so much? They've got the same pent-up energy that we've found an outlet for.

In the last few years, I've discovered that stitching with the television off is even more relaxing. I won't stay with it as long, though. If I really want to get a project finished, starting a movie is the best way to keep me in my seat. If I've seen and enjoyed the movie before, more than half of my brain will concentrate on my stitching. I'll stay to see my favorite parts and pick up things I missed before, but I won't get so caught up in the movie that I'll discover my work left neglected in my lap.

However, if I'm stressed, sitting in a quiet room with my current needlecraft project will relax me more quickly and thoroughly than watching television. In fact, I've fallen asleep knitting, just like I might while reading.

Situations that hold the possibility of additional stress make our stitchery projects even more important. I have one project ready to grab and take with me to doctors' offices and any other place where I am likely to have to sit and wait. I find that people assume I must be in a terrible hurry to finish some particular project if I'm taking it everywhere I go. That's hardly ever the case. I'm just trying to keep my hands and my brain busy so I don't think about how long I've been waiting. I'll take projects that can be stuffed back in my bag at a moment's notice, leaving counted cross-stitch projects at home because of the need to constantly refer to the pattern and sometimes the picture as well.

I also like to take my stitchery with me on car trips, to make the time when I'm not driving go faster. Here I avoid knitting for fear of what the needles might do to me or someone else in the car in the event of an accident. Crochet hooks are, perhaps, even more dangerous. Embroidery and small quilting projects seem ideal for me. I'll sometimes have two projects with me on vacations: one for actual travel and a larger or more complex one for the hotel room.

Recent new regulations have made it difficult to take sewing projects along if you're flying. I've had a pair of thread scissors confiscated even though the blade was only an inch long. I was told that round-pointed scissors, such as baby fingernail scissors, would make it through. Also, I think the sewing supply industry is now making round-pointed thread scissors. I've been relying instead on the little round medallions with the blade encased inside. You can even wear them around your neck so they are always handy. You cut your thread at the tiny openings in the filigree where the blade is exposed. There are few things more frustrating than being stuck in an airport while your flight is delayed. If you can spend the time doing something creative, you can almost enjoy it.

Needle Pointers

I bet you've been underestimating the importance of your needlecraft hobby. My daughter, Eden, tells me that she has alluded to her cross-stitching experience in job interviews as an example of detail-oriented work.

Job hunting aside, several people have reported arriving at a meditative state while stitching. Minor physical pain can be forgotten and problems are set aside. The stress relief actually lasts beyond the sewing session, sort of like a hot shower on sore muscles. Dorothy Grant, the woman who needlepointed while her husband watched sports, said that her mother used needlework to battle Parkinson's disease; her mother claimed that a few minutes of stitching calmed her hands down. Probably it relieved the stress that was affecting the disease.

Likewise, meditating on our hobby can relieve stress at other times. Try to confine this to appropriate settings so that you don't lose your job or run your car into something. A recent opportunity to stretch my creative imagination followed a fall that resulted in a broken kneecap. In the subsequent months I had three MRIs taken of the knee to try to determine how much damage had been done to the tendon and how it was healing.

The MRI machine is sort of a tunnel you're slid into. Fortunately for me, I didn't have to go in so far that my head was inside or I might have been too claustrophobic to think of much else. Once the imaging starts you aren't supposed to move, talk, twitch, or otherwise show any signs of life for thirty minutes or so. The only thing that can be active is your brain.

Mine planned sewing projects. I could make a quilt with small 9-patches that alternated yellow fabric and blue fabric. These blocks could be paired with fabrics of blue and yellow print, alternating lights and darks. That would mean larger 4-patches made up of two 9-patches and two light blocks alternating with 4-patches made of two darks and two lights.

Or that blue picture print I couldn't use for a project last year could be fussy-cut to show off the pictures and surrounded by smaller squares split into dark blue and white triangles, sort of like flying geese between the pictures. Since some pictures are larger than others, there would need to be more "geese" surrounding some pictures. I hate sewing with triangles! Do I really want to do this? But it would be really awesome if I did.

Maybe I want to use up some of my green marbled print on another turtle. I love my quilted-back turtle with the embroidered eyes. How hard would it be to make a snail? Is there any chance I could find a pattern for a snail? Or could I simply draw a spiral shell and make two, quilting them, of course. Then I would need some kind of strip over the top to give it three dimensions. The snail body would be a bit tricky.

Wouldn't it be clever to convert some of Picasso's line draw-ings to embroidery motifs? I saved a calendar of his drawings a few years ago that would make a good resource. Or maybe I could find some of John Lennon's drawings if I want to get a bit bizarre.

I'm not sure I made any definite sewing plans, other than that yellow and blue quilt, but it sure helped the time go by faster and kept me from obsessing on the pain that developed in my lower back after five minutes of lying on the hard table.

If I can't sleep, I sometimes count projects instead of sheep. If I come to one I've set aside because I don't know how to proceed, I try to solve the problem. The more complicated the problem, the more likely it is to put me to sleep. Some night I'm going to dream of sewing, but if I have, I can't remember. My dream dictionary suggests that if you dream of sewing, par-ticularly mending, you have a hurt or tear in a relationship that you want to mend. Or your dream of stitching may mean that you want to change some old habit or create a new attitude. If I dream of sewing, I'll assume I've been a bit preoccupied with my favorite hobby.

The Legacy

It's hard to say when embroidery and all the other forms of decorative stitching generally referred to as stitchery first started. Historians believe that its most rudimentary form pre-dates painting. We know that needlepoint has been found in

Egyptian pharaohs' tombs. The earliest written record of Chinese embroidery is in the *Shangshu* (Book of History) compiled between 1027 and 771 B.C. Needlepoint and cross-stitch were common in the Roman Empire and there are several references to embroidery in Homer's *Iliad* and *Odyssey,* written around 500 B.C., including references to an embroidered depiction of the Trojan Wars done by Helen of Troy herself. And, of course, there is the Bayeux Tapestry, dating to sometime after A.D 1066.

Embroidery and related arts seem to have developed all over the world, sometimes independently, sometimes borrowing from one another because of either trade or conquest. Embroidery probably began as embellishments for garments, then expanded into decorations for temples and churches and finally homes of rulers and eventually of common folk as well.

In the Middle Ages, needlework seems to have been one of the few acceptable activities for noblewomen. Many church records mention altar cloths and the like donated by queens and other noblewomen, often adding "made by her own hands."

In convents, embroidery was encouraged as long as it didn't interfere with worship. Evidently a few of these women enjoyed stitchery a bit too much. An ecclesiastical council held in 747 recommended more reading of books and singing of songs and less needlework. It was evidently a theme that came up again and again. Most of us can understand how stitchery can become an obsession.

Embroidery's greatest days were probably between 1250 and 1350. Opus Anglicanum (English embroidery) became much sought after all over Europe. This was the age of countless needlework schools, guilds, and workshops, large and small.

Other countries had their specialties, too. There was trapunto in Italy and counted-thread embroideries in Scandinavia that went back to the Viking era. Germans perfected a pulled-thread technique, a forerunner of Hardanger lace.

The plague of 1348, which killed nearly half of England's population, and the political upheavals that followed had a negative effect on the needlecraft trade. So did the increase in the manufacture of brocade fabrics. But as the guilds and shops closed their doors, embroidery and needlepoint moved into the homes and evolved to fill the desires and styles of the times as they changed.

In a sense, we modern needlecrafters are indebted to all those who went before us, refining and developing the tools and techniques of the diverse crafts that make up needlework. My personal appreciation of that legacy is expressed in my thimble collection. Not the decorative ones sold at tourist attractions, though I like those, too. The collection I treasure includes the working thimbles that belonged to Joe's grandmother, my aunt Lois, my mother, and even the one my father used after Mom's death forced him to learn to sew on his own buttons. There's even a tiny thimble I used as a kid.

No Idle Hands

I suspect that many of us were first taught to wield a needle and thread as a way of keeping us busy. The usual age, for those of us who were taught as children, seems to be around six. Most six-year-olds are going to be quickly bored with toys that they enjoyed a year or so before. Yet most of them aren't yet able to read. They want to do something new, something grown-up. Getting them started with a needle and thread can give Mom a few minutes of peace.

There are many stories of children, boys as well as girls, learning to sew, knit, or crochet because they were confined to bed recovering from an illness. As recently as fifty or sixty years ago, bed rest was about the only thing a doctor could prescribe for some illnesses. The recommended time in bed would have been longer than now, as well. You can imagine the difficulty of keeping an active child in bed after the worst symptoms had passed. In the time before television and video games, moms had quite a challenge finding things for a child to do while following the doctor's orders.

When my youngest son was two, he spent several weeks in the Kansas University Medical Center being treated for leukemia. He was easily occupied with all the toys in the playroom, but another patient, ten-year-old James, was not and neither was I. I had purchased three small needlepoint kits from the hospital gift shop to keep myself busy while I watched Paul play, and I let James work on one of them whenever we happened to be in the playroom at the same time. Basic needlepoint is simple enough that he didn't have any trouble picking up the technique. His mother found us there once and was afraid her son would ruin my needlepoint. I don't think I completely convinced her that the projects were just something to do, like a puzzle or playing solitaire. I would have been happy to let James keep the one he worked on, but he always gave it back to me when he tired of it. While it never held his attention very long (I doubt if I turned him into a devoted needlecrafter), it was something different to do.

Those three kits, along with all those tea towels I embroidered as a kid and most of the projects I've had in my take-along bag, are projects more for the sake of doing than of having. This is probably true of a large percentage of needlecrafts that are made in homes today. Perhaps it's been that way for a long time. From early colonial days to more than fifty years after the American Revolution, girls were taught to embroider as part of—in some cases, almost the entirety of—their formal education.

America was strongly influenced by the Puritans, who believed that idle hands were the devil's workshop. If one didn't have something constructive to do, one would get into trouble. Women, they felt, were especially susceptible to the devil's influence, and while one would think that there would have been plenty in the way of housework, gardening, sewing, mending, spinning, weaving, and child-rearing to keep a woman busy, she was still required to learn fancywork to fill up those occasional idle minutes.

An article by Olive Blair Graffam in the September/ October 2003 issue of *Piecework* magazine describes some of the early girls' schools and the significance of studying the resulting "schoolgirl art" as a way of understanding the attitudes of the time. Some of these schools took girls as young as two, making them sound more like neighborhood day cares than schools.

The "samplers" of today date back to this period or before. In the 1700s, a sampler would nearly always include the alphabet, much as they do today. They might include both capital and lowercase letters, sometimes done in more than one style. They were often decorated with pictures, such as birds or baskets of fruit or flowers. The notion was that the samplers would teach several stitches and the alphabet at the same time. Also popular in these schools were decorated sayings, generally religious or patriotic, that were intended to reinforce moral behavior as well.

Some historians question whether these young girls were actually learning to read or whether they were merely copying the stitch patterns provided by their teacher. Reading, beyond what was needed to run a household, was considered by some to be unnecessary or even dangerous for women anyway.

While I'm certainly glad that attitudes toward girls' education have changed, I would love to have had stitchery as part of my grade school curriculum. Even a suggestion that it was an alternative to the games I was humiliatingly bad at during recess would have been welcome. I remember that my teacher broke her foot when I was in the first grade and her daughter came and taught us for a few days until our teacher could get around a little better. The daughter was expecting her first child and spent most of the time crocheting a blanket, which I found much more interesting than my reading or math.

There are some wonderful samplers preserved from the Colonial era. The young stitcher often put her age as well as her name on them. Six and seven are not uncommon ages. I was stitching away on my own at that age, though nothing I did was really worth preserving, including the one tea towel I did preserve. But after reading about these stitchery schools in the article mentioned and in Laurel Thatcher Ulrich's book *The Age of Homespun*, I've begun fantasizing about making a chimneypiece. Girls who excelled in needlework and whose parents could afford to continue to send them to school eventually made a piece intended to hang above the fireplace that might be three or four feet across. It was sort of their master's thesis in needlecraft. Often these were drawn by the instructor and contained several scenes, mostly what we might consider pastoral or romanticized images of daily life. Sometimes these scenes were clearly borrowed from famous works of art, and they weren't necessarily in proper perspective with each other. But they showed off the stitcher's skill with a needle.

I think one of these would be a lot of fun. Since I have no skill whatsoever with a pencil, my design will have to be borrowed from something as well. I think it would be a challenge to include as many different kinds of stitches as possible. Regular needlepoint doesn't generally mix too well with embroidery, but I can see using it as a border. Every plain and fancy embroidery stitch could be included as well as some beadwork and stumpwork, maybe even ribbon embroidery.

Now this, if I ever do it, will definitely qualify as a Zen project. Even though I haven't found the right picture (or pictures) to copy, I have trouble imagining it as anything I'd really want to display except maybe occasionally. I do, in fact, have a fireplace, the appropriate location of a chimneypiece. My problem is that I'm afraid it'll be a hodgepodge of stitches, yarns, and materials. Perhaps that can be my challenge: distribute enough of the more dramatic effects of stumpwork, which is truly three-dimensional, and any beads or ribbons over the piece to create some continuity.

But even picturing the outcome as a worst-case scenario doesn't dampen my enthusiasm for the whole idea. Maybe it's the scope of the project that has me excited. Or maybe it's just the size. Imagine the stir in a doctor's office if I pulled out a three-by-four foot piece of canvas to embroider.

My ideas may change several times before I settle on what I want to do, but right now I'm toying with the idea of designing my piece like an antique map. One from around 1800 seems appropriate, since it would be consistent with the greatest popularity of chimneypieces. Maps in those days showed more than landmasses. They were generally highly decorated, sometimes with whales, ships, and even mythological creatures. This would give me more possibilities for creative stitching.

At this point, with the idea barely formed in my mind, I see the whole thing as a bit of a test to see if I can envision such a large work, then actually pull it off. I wonder how the young women of the late 1700s and early 1800s saw their chimneypieces. Somewhat the same, I imagine. These were to be their masterpieces, so to speak—the works that showed their tutors that they had mastered the various skills they had set out to learn.

Because I will choose and draw (somehow) my own picture, I will have more creative control than these young women did. Even though it is of my own making, it is control nevertheless. I will want to balance that control with spontaneity as I stitch.

Sometimes those spur-of-the-moment decisions to stray from the original plan are the things that bring a peace to life.

And when I actually get started on this project, I know that it will be completely absorbing, which is probably why I think about it with such anticipation. I don't want to start it now, because I have several major commitments right now, including this book. At the same time, I know I can't wait until *everything* is done and I have all the time in the world. That will never happen. My guess is that I'll find sometime in between. Balance again. I'll settle on a picture, buy the supplies, and find a time when it just seems right to begin.

 Try This

Make something for yourself that honors your creativity. Needlework a picture that represents another hobby. Make a needle book or pincushion or a sewing bag for travel projects. Work up an appliqué that represents another hobby and sew it to a sweatshirt, jacket, pillow, or tote bag. If you're feeling more ambitious, make a wall hanging or pillow top that is a collage of all the different creative things you do. This can be done with themed fabrics, appliqué, embroidery, or a combination of them all. As you work, remind yourself that your creativity is a gift and the best way to say thanks is to use it.

chapter ten

Back to the Beginning

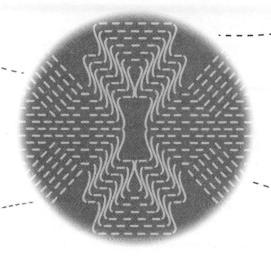

Tip: Interfacing

Interfacing stiffens or stabilizes fabric. In garment construction it is used in cuffs, collars, and waistbands, and behind buttons and buttonholes. You can use solid color fabric for interfacing, but regular interfacing works better. Fusible interfacing is usually the easiest to work with. Iron the fabric piece to the interfacing, then cut the interfacing out around the fabric. Interfacing is handy for backing appliqué, making it easier both to cut out intricate pieces and to sew them to the background fabric. You can use fusible interfacing to back embroidery work on delicate fabrics. If you are making your own construction pattern, try using regular interfacing instead of paper.

Back to School

Recently I attended a trapunto class. Trapunto, also called Italian embroidery, is really a form of quilting. Traditionally it involves working intricate quilting stitches through two layers of solid-color fabric, then carefully inserting stuffing or cord through the backing fabric so that some areas in the quilting pattern are raised.

The class was taught by Kathy Delaney, author of several books on appliqué. Ms. Delaney taught a clever method of basting a thick layer of batting to the underside of your marked top layer of fabric in those areas you want stuffed, thus stuffing your project before you quilt the layers together. You then quilt very densely in the areas outside these raised areas, making them stand out even more. She describes the technique in the October 2004 issue of *Quilters Newsletter Magazine*.

I drove about fifty miles to a little town in Nebraska to attend the class. It was sponsored by a quilt guild that is sort of a sister guild to the one I attend across the border south in Kansas. There were members from both guilds in attendance, but since I had only joined my own guild a few months earlier, I saw familiar faces but no one I really knew.

Some of the conversation as we set out our supplies and waited for more quilters to arrive centered on other classes we had attended or taught, and particularly on people who had made the class less than enjoyable, students who argued with the teacher or teachers who made some students feel inferior. The stories were told with a sense of humor, however. While

Ms. Delaney claimed she felt more pressure to be a good teacher, her participation in the exchange had actually made her seem more approachable.

She had several of her appliqué books available for sale if we wanted to convert appliqué patterns for use with trapunto. She also had some very simple patterns available for free. We should start with a small project, she said, to find out if we liked it.

That is wonderful advice, the kind I would probably give and almost never take. I didn't take it that day either. I already had a big project planned, a floral wall hanging. I decided I wanted to do four trapunto blocks about 10" by 18" each. I would sew them together after they were quilted. I knew a couple of ways to do that and had decided which I wanted to try. The plan was, and is, to sew the blocks together *wrong* sides facing, trim the seam allowances, especially the batting, and cover the remaining raw edges with a print fabric that complemented the quilted designs. The only problem I foresee is at the very center, where the thick seams cross, but I'll cross that bridge when I come to it.

When I bought the materials for the class, I bought enough for four blocks and cut everything accordingly. Before the class started, while the others were sharing their war stories, I looked through her books, found one that was full of patterns just like I'd envisioned, and bought it. I was just about ready to start without her when she offered that bit of sage advice: "Start small until you know if you like it."

Now, if the moral of this little tale is supposed to be to follow that advice, I'd be in trouble. I don't have any terrible catastrophe to report. I haven't tired of the project and stored it all away.

I'm well into quilting the second block and still as delighted with it as I was when I first signed up for the class.

Of course, I knew enough about trapunto to know that it would be mostly hand quilting. I already know that I like to do that. I figured that this would be a good project to have ready to take with me when I know there's a chance I'll be sitting and waiting somewhere. This project, because it's hand-worked in four small pieces, is very portable.

However, I didn't know exactly how our teacher was going to have us stuff some areas of the blocks or even what I was going to find in the way of designs for the quilting stitches. I guess I just wanted to plunge in instead of dipping my toes. A larger project would give me a chance to practice enough that I'd really know if I liked it or not. Too small a project, such as a pillow top, might be finished before I really got the hang of it.

I took a tatting class once. Tatting looks a little like crochet, but the technique is altogether different. Traditional tatting involves a shuttle, but this class taught a method using a long needle. We learned the basic steps but did not have an actual project to do. I mastered the technique in class, but with nothing to continue working on, I quickly forgot. Now I find that even the written instructions make no sense. I needed to use the technique a great many more times right away to really learn it.

Still, even though I am just doing a wall hanging, not a full-sized quilt, I could have been biting off more than I could chew. Many years ago, I wanted to see if I could make a Cathedral Window quilt. I didn't want a pillow top or a table runner. I wanted a full-sized quilt. Cathedral Windows are made by folding the corners of 6" squares of plain fabric into the center twice, and then sewing these smaller, folded squares together. Next you sew 2" printed squares on point across the seams and use the folds from the earlier step to cover the raw edges of the smaller squares. It took me a few dozen squares to get the hang of it and several dozen more for it to get really boring. Unfortunately, it takes several hundred squares to make a full-sized quilt. All the pieces rested in a drawer for years and years, coming out occasionally for a few weeks before returning to their place of exile. I finished the quilt about twenty years after I started it.

One would think I wouldn't make the same mistake again, but I've started a Mosaic quilt. It involves hand-piecing together a few hundred hexagons of less than 3" diameter. It's no big surprise that that gets a little boring. Maybe my goal for completion should be 2022! That chimneypiece I'm contemplating may well be another example.

But I also remembered the tatting class and wanted to avoid making a sample of trapunto that I would file away with the instructions. There may be some pride involved, here, I realize. I don't want to come home from class with a tiny sample of trapunto as if it were some craft from camp. I wanted a real project.

There's got to be something in between a project so small that you don't give yourself a chance to really learn something new and a project so large that you have trouble finishing it. Some balance, so to speak. For me that's a wall hanging. Here's where knowing yourself is going to come in handy. When starting any new project, consider your tenacity and attention span as well as the amount of sewing time you have available. Also, how big a desire you have for the finished project will influence both of these things.

However, if you love to sew, not all of your projects are going to be for a practical purpose. We may feel we need an excuse to learn something new, so we tell ourselves that we have a use for it when we're done. If all else fails, we can say that we'll use it as a gift.

In fact, it's probably better to have a use in mind when you start something new. That desire for the finished project can go a long way toward keeping you going if you hit a snag. But that's not why I took the trapunto class.

Those of us who sign up for sewing or stitchery classes, especially those classes that teach us how to make one particular thing, don't do it because we happen to need whatever it is that's being taught. If we did, we'd just go out and buy it. We sign up for the joy of discovery. We sign up to sew with friends or to make new friends. We sign up because hobbies are supposed to be fun and the class sounds fun.

Tension Control

My friend Nancy Collins has attended the quilting retreats offered by Sister Betty Suther at Manna House of Prayer. Manna House is a spiritual center operated by the Sisters of St. Joseph of Concordia, Kansas. Many different kinds of retreats are held there. While I've twice attended the "quilter's choice" retreat in which we all bring whatever we're working on for a weekend of intensive sewing, Nancy signs up for the instructional retreats. Sister Betty picks a pattern and teaches those attending how to make it. Nancy doesn't know exactly what she's going to make until she gets the list of necessary supplies, which includes the pattern. Clearly, she isn't signing up because she has a need for the finished product.

When I decided on my trapunto project, did I need something else to hang on my wall? Not really, though I will enjoy it in my living room. Did I need a new project? Oh, heavens, no! I just wanted to do it, purely for the experience.

Creativity could be defined as the balance between spontaneity and control. If you remember, the first of the three goals of Zen practice is to balance and unify the mind in exactly this way. Balance is always a bit tricky. It's like yin and yang, two equal but opposite forces. In sewing, too much spontaneity and the pieces won't fit, the end result won't be pleasing, or you may find yourself sewn into a corner, so to speak, and unable to finish. Too much control and there is no originality, nothing that makes the finished product really yours. Think of it like the tension on your sewing machine. The right setting for your thread and fabric will mean that your stitches are exactly alike on the top and the underside of your seam. If the tension is too tight or too loose, one side will show loops of thread from the other side.

On the other hand, when you're learning something new, you have to give up a bit of your spontaneity in favor of enough control to actually learn something. In fact, in a sense you turn control over to someone else, whether that's a classroom teacher or another person whose written instruction you are following.

The temptation might be to skip a new, unfamiliar step and substitute an alternative method that you're already familiar with. Your end product may be similar to the instructor's, but you've missed an opportunity.

You've also let preconceived notions of what is easiest keep you from seeing reality clearly: a new, different method or skill that's being presented to you. It's a little like finding a new recipe but not going to the store for the exotic ingredients. Can you really say you've tried the new recipe if you substitute half the ingredients? Could I really say I learned trapunto if I decided to simply quilt my layers together without the additional padding? It would still be a pretty wall hanging, but I wouldn't have learned anything new.

Having Beginner's Mind, even after years of stitching, will help you to be open to these learning experiences. Some studies have suggested that learning new things is a possible way of battling Alzheimer's disease. New skills learned build new pathways in your brain, bypassing the tangled pathways caused by the disease. If you needed another excuse to take that class you've been wanting to sign up for, there it is. Tell your spouse—and yourself—that you are signing up for medical reasons.

Tension Release

When you are learning something new, it's difficult to think about anything else, your mind is so involved with what you are doing. Problems that preoccupy you the rest of the time slip away. Recently, more and more people have discovered the therapeutic value of learning sewing and other crafts. Part of it is a desire for a relaxed social gathering, certainly, but a lot of it is the absorbing nature of the craft itself. *The New York Times* ran an article on February 24, 2004, entitled "Needle Trades Provide Therapy" by Ruth LaFerla. She describes a sewing class as a refuge and comments on the wide diversity in age and occupation of those in attendance.

Needlecrafts, particularly quilting, cross-stitch, and knitting, are growing in popularity as people realize that their creative instinct needs an outlet. The finished product is generally of small consideration. This desire to do something for the experience itself is very Zen.

Creativity makes you feel especially alive. All your senses come into play, including your reasoning, which in Zen practice is considered one of the six senses. The deep concentration and the necessary mindfulness as you work can result in an experience akin to enlightenment, the second goal of Zen. Eventually you learn enough that part of every sewing project—even all of some—will seem routine. When there is nothing new to learn with a particular project, your concentration changes. Perhaps the original high is gone, and you set the project aside as I did with the Cathedral Window. But if you can stay with it, sewing at your own rhythm, sewing can become a form of working meditation. The repetition of the activity is like the repetition of a phrase or chant used to calm the wandering mind in sitting meditation. This sounds like another koan. Mindfulness leads to mindlessness.

The more you let your conscious mind center on your sewing, staying mindful of your sewing, the more you allow your subconscious mind to wander, like Ann at the factory. If you are not
being called upon to solve a problem with your sewing, you might
discover your mind solving one of those problems your sewing
seemed to let you forget. Mindlessness leads back to mindfulness.

Several avid needlecrafter friends have told me of this type
of thing happening. The dilemmas and their solutions were personal enough that they didn't want to share the details, but the
experiences were significant. One even interpreted the solution
as a message from God.

My own experiences with this phenomenon have been a little less dramatic—small household decisions and the like. Back
when I was writing fiction, I'd occasionally solve my plot dilemmas while I was avoiding my writing by pursuing one of my hobbies. I've also solved quilt-pattern dilemmas when I was trying to
write. This is probably a misuse of mindlessness.

My preoccupation with my hobby at the expense of my
occupation aside, this mindlessness is more likely to happen
when I'm sewing something repetitious, such as a large section
of needlepoint, row after row of plain knitting or thirty-five identical blocks for a quilt top. My concentration is not needed for the
hows or whats of the pattern at this point. I'm only concerned
that my stitches are even. I sew quilt blocks in an assembly-
line fashion. I chain-piece—that is, feed one pair of pieces
under the needle directly after the last. I sew a particular step
for all the blocks, press all the seams, and move on to the next
step. Unfortunately, if I sew something wrong on one block, I'll

probably do the same on all of them, as I recently did on one of my Bear's Paw baby quilts. The poor bear is pigeon-toed.

Still, this type of sewing is peaceful work—similar, I'm sure, to the feelings one would have at a loom, passing the shuttle back and forth at a smooth, comfortable rhythm.

Even if no great insight flashes into my mind, I'm refreshed by the experience. The unhurried but steady pace stays with me when I set the project aside to fix dinner or go about whatever needs to be done. I have been calmed by the simple repetition of my stitching. I'm reminded of the old nursery rhyme:

Crosspatch, draw the latch,
Sit by the fire and spin;
Take a cup and drink it up,
Then call your neighbors in.

The subject of the rhyme is spinning rather than sewing but it would be equally repetitious. She's gone from cross to inviting her neighbors in because of a session of spinning. Of course, we don't know what was in the cup.

Returning to my office job on Monday after a weekend at a quilting retreat was almost surreal. I felt completely different than I had on Friday. I felt unflappable. I don't know if my change of attitude was visible to anyone else or exactly how long it lasted, but it made me want to attend quilting retreats more than just once a year.

I talked my daughter into attending one with me this past year. I started planning on it while I was at the retreat the year before. Eden was game, but she wasn't sure she would want to

spend *that* much time sewing. She came to my house and we
went in together early Friday evening. Because she wanted to
spend some time with her daddy, too, we had not taken rooms
at Manna House but went home about 9:00 P.M.

We took separate cars into town on Saturday morning
because she didn't think she'd be as eager to get an early start
as I would. She slept later than I did, visited with her dad, and
joined me in town about midmorning. Then she really got into
sewing. On Sunday morning I left my bedroom, thinking I was
up fairly early, only to find her sitting at the dining room table
ready to go. I'm surprised she didn't leave without me. The
retreat ended at noon on Sunday. We came home, set up our
machines, and sewed for another couple of hours.

Eye of the Needle

This change of mood after sewing doesn't always happen, of
course. If your stresses are great enough, you'll have difficulty
connecting with your sewing project or any other hobby. It
becomes work, rather than play. I swear the embroidery floss
tangles more if I'm tense or hurried. As my daughter likes to
say after she had a lot of trouble getting a quilt's binding to lie
smooth, "Don't sew angry." At the time when you most need
the benefits of your hobby, the ability to enjoy it deserts you.

A conscious effort toward Beginner's Mind can help you.
Try to see your project as if it were new. You can't actually go
back, but try to remember how you felt when you first learned a

particular skill. If that is lost in your childhood, imagine that you are explaining it all to someone else. This gives you an opportunity to see your sewing from another point of view, through the eyes of your imagined student. Seeing the techniques through new eyes gives you a new perspective and renews the joy.

If you have the temperament and the time, you might consider teaching for real. Of course, all may not always go smoothly. My 4-H sewing leader, Mariesther Holbert, taught an adult class to make wool suits. When she was preparing the lapel of the suit jacket to show her class she managed to scorch the fabric with her iron. She was more upset with herself than she would have been with any of her students. She was supposed to be the teacher!

She used everything she could think of to minimize the damage. She couldn't get rid of it entirely, but the garment was usable in the end. She shared the experience with her students, and they all had a good laugh. I imagine that the students were glad to learn from her mistake rather than making it themselves.

If you don't want the pressure of a structured class, perhaps you could volunteer to teach a young relative or neighbor child. Be sure you keep your expectations realistic and age appropriate. If you find yourself getting frustrated, imagine how your young student must feel.

If your mind can accept outlandish ideas without feeling too foolish, try seeing your project from the point of view of the cloth or yarn. If the universe is all one, as the Buddhists say, you and the project are part of the same and the separation is only imagined. Think about that as you stitch and see if it eases the tedium.

If you find yourself regularly experiencing a lack of interest in a once-loved hobby, it could be a sign of depression. Seek help if you need it and follow your doctor or counselor's advice. Often that advice will include doing something you used to like to do. You may need to force yourself at first, but your love for your hobby can help you regain your joy for life. As you try to get your life back on track, remember that Zen is interested in now and where you go from here. This includes how we work with suffering. "Why?" is not a reasonable question, because there is no answer. Zen is concerned with this moment.

A Soul That Soars

There's a special pleasure in designing my own projects. It involves a level of concentration and imagination beyond what I experience simply following a pattern or set of instructions. Most of us have to do a lot of direction-following first, but once we've learned the rules and techniques, we can't help but start modifying things.

It feels a bit risky plunging into something completely original. Having a pattern as a basis to build our own creation on is a little like having a safety net. It makes us feel confident enough to explore our own creativity, where starting cold makes us cautious.

Our first changes may seem so minor that we don't consider them in terms of self-expression or originality. We're only making a pattern work for us. This is what we're doing when we alter a clothing pattern to fit, revise a cross-stitch pattern to suit our tastes, or change a drapery pattern, as Jane Snavely does, to make it fit a window and the customer's expectation.

And this is what Karla McMillan did when she made all of her daughter's formal dresses for the prom and other special occasions. Since she was never able to find a pattern exactly like what Ashley wanted, she would buy the pattern that was closest and alter it. To test her new pattern, Karla made a dress out of a cheap fabric. Once Ashley used a trial dress as a sundress, but most of the time the practice dresses were made out of some odd material. They were primarily Karla's safety net when making these high-stress dresses.

At first glance it might seem as if Karla, Jane, and I aren't being as original as we might be. But everyone, scientists and artists alike, builds on other people's work. There's little use, as they say, in reinventing the wheel. In fact, getting the technical aspects of the pattern out of the way can let you get to the creative part sooner, before frustrations with armhole curves or drawing our own picture for cross-stitch have made you abandon the project.

When we free our creativity, we become most honestly ourselves. We can dismiss the preconceived notions of how someone else would do it and live most clearly in the moment. That balancing act of spontaneity and self-control becomes second nature and we give ourselves over to that superalertness that is also part of Zen practice.

For the time that we are lost in our hobby, we are able to rise above the difficulties of our lives and see things in perspective. Plato said, "The perfect soul soars upward and brings order to the whole world." With our surrender to our creative selves comes a sense of order—to our own little portion of the world, at least.

If you can replace a few more of those rules that you've worked so hard to learn and follow with the urgings of your own imagination, you'll feel more creative and have a stronger feeling of authorship of your finished product. You'll also be able to detach yourself a little more thoroughly from those burdens that are tying you down.

There are also rules outside the guidelines of sewing that tend to limit us. We make most of these rules ourselves, some out of necessity, others out of habit or long-forgotten instruction. Sometimes our restrictions are completely subconscious until we examine them. (More of that introspection, again.) It's true that rules orient us, but they also can limit us.

Look at the things you've been sewing lately and see if you've put restrictions on the kinds and colors of fabric or yarn you'll allow yourself to use, the types of garments or crafts you're willing to try, or the amount of time you're willing to devote to a single project. Perhaps one big, challenging project might be more satisfying than three small ones.

The cost of the materials might be a necessary restriction as well. But sometimes we pass up the more expensive fabric, telling ourselves that we don't really deserve it, then spend the same amount of money on a magazine or on treats that we don't really want as much as that beautiful fabric we shied away from.

As you increasingly leave the guidelines and your earlier restrictions behind, making your sewing projects more and more your own, you may discover a need to set a different kind of restriction on your sewing. Exactly how many projects will you allow yourself to start before you have to finish something?

When you engage your own creativity in the planning of a project, you may discover that that phase, while you're still trying out your new idea, is much more exhilarating than the construction itself. This tends to make some of us want to always be starting something new. Leonardo da Vinci, famous for the *Mona Lisa* and the *Last Supper*, was notorious for leaving work unfinished. He wrote in his journal that planning a piece is divine; executing it is slavery.

I recently joined a quilters' guild. In welcoming me, the president said, "We have all kinds of quilters here. There are beginners . . . and there are finishers." She, it seems, is a beginner. The running joke is that she often brings something newly begun for show and tell but never brings a finished quilt. Another avid needlecrafter told me that once she counted up all her unfinished projects and found there were seventy! I trail way behind with somewhere between twenty and twenty-five. Zen teaches that the universe is one mind that expresses itself in many different ways. Some of us have universe-like minds all by ourselves.

It's also not uncommon for people who have freed their creativity to discover other outlets. Needlecrafts may or may not be the first creative activity to enthrall you. It's often the one that complements the others in some way. We discover that we can sew for our other hobbies.

I love knitting as well as construction sewing, so I made a lining for a bushel basket with multitiered pockets to store my knitting supplies. The back tier holds the straight needles. In front of that is a row of wider pockets for circular needles. A third row of pockets holds double-pointed needles and other accessories. I made a packet for crochet hooks that rolls up and a little book with pockets for tapestry needles, which I store in the center of the basket. Besides the joy of sewing something original that required a meditative level of creativity, I ended up with a finished project that enhanced another creative endeavor.

As with anything else, when we do any needlecraft, we bring all of our past experiences with us. Some of these experiences help us build toward more creative expression. Others limit us and need to be dismissed in favor of the here and now. What we stitch and how we do it is karma, the logical outcome of cause and effect of all these past experiences and how we let them affect us.

No one else will make exactly the same choices you do. Your finished project will be uniquely yours. At the same time, you share a bond with other seamstresses, tailors, knitters, and embroiderers past, present, and future. And spinners and weavers, too. This bond can help you recognize the oneness of the whole world and your particular place in it. It's so much more than simply working needle and thread.

When my son Paul returned home after his National Guard unit had been deployed in Bosnia, he brought me a beautifully embroidered dresser scarf. He said he bought it from a woman in a little shop. Even after growing up around me and all my needlecraft projects, he couldn't tell by looking at the piece if it was actually hand-stitched or not. The woman told him she had made it herself, but he knew she might have just been wanting to make a sale. "But," he observed, "she handled it like she had made it." Now where do you suppose he learned that?

 Try This

Learn something new. Sign up for a class or buy a how-to book. Choose something you've always wanted to do but thought was too difficult. Be reasonable and sign up for the beginner classes, but take the plunge into something new. And bring a friend.

Tote Bag for Beginners

One of the simplest and most versatile projects for a beginner is a tote bag. There are no complicated steps, you're sewing straight seams and everything can be cut by measure. Best of all, you can make it any shape or size you want and decorate it to your heart's content. However, if you aren't interested in construction sewing and want to go straight to the decorating, plain tote bags are available at most craft stores.

The instructions that follow are for a small bag, 15" wide and 15" deep. This is small enough that it won't be necessary to reinforce the bottom, but large enough for books or most crafts. If you want to make a larger bag, adjust the pattern accordingly.

Fabrics

For the size mentioned above, you'll need ⅔ yard of a heavy woven fabric. Some stretch on the diagonal is to be expected, but reject any fabric that stretches either lengthwise or cross-wise or your bag will stretch out of shape when you use it. Canvas or heavy broadcloth is recommended. Denim is great if it isn't so heavy that it's difficult to work with. Replace your sewing machine needle with one designed for heavy fabrics. Choose a solid-color fabric so you can decorate the front to reflect your creativity.

If you anticipate washing your bag at any time in the future, wash the fabric before you cut out the pieces. If washing softened the cloth appreciably, use some spray starch when you iron it. Straighten one cut edge of your fabric by pulling a thread and cutting in the line left behind. If your fabric has an obvious enough weave, you may be able to cut along a thread without pulling it.

Fold the fabric along this cut edge with the selvages, those tightly woven finished sides of your fabric, together and hold it up. If the selvages do not hang in a straight line, tug the fabric along the diagonal, called the bias, to straighten the fabric.

Cutting

Begin by cutting away the selvages. They tend to shrink and you'll find it easier to cut the pieces accurately once they are gone.

Measure down 4" from the cut edge and follow another thread across, or use an acrylic ruler and rotary cutter to cut a 4" strip the entire length of the fabric. Cut this strip in half at the center fold of the fabric to make two strips 4" by approximately 22". These will be the handles of your bag.

Next cut a piece 16" by 31". This will be the body of the tote bag. If you fold the fabric with the cut edges in line, you can cut through two layers at once. The fabric fold will be the bottom of the bag. If you picked a fabric with a one-way design, you'll need to cut two pieces 16" by 16" and sew them together at the bottom to avoid having your pattern upside down on the back.

From the remaining fabric, cut two strips 3½" by 16". These will be the facing pieces for the top.

Making the Straps

Fold the 4" strips in half the long way with the right side of the fabric together. Stitch along the entire length ½" from the raw edge. Leave the ends open. Press one layer of the seam allowance away from the other to make it easier to separate the seam allowances once they are inside your turned handle.

Fasten a large safety pin to the seam allowance near one end of a strap. Tuck the pin inside and use it to turn the handle right side out by gathering it along to the other end. Do the same with the other handle.

Now your straps need to be pressed flat. If your fabric will cooperate, press them so the seam is in the center of one side of the handle with the seam allowance open inside the handle. If this is too difficult, simply press the handles flat with the seam along one edge. Roll the seam a little between your fingers to get it opened as neatly as possible.

Set these pieces aside along with the facing pieces.

Decorating the Bag

Now is the time to get creative. The following are suggestions rather than instructions. Look through them and see what strikes your interest, or come up with something else altogether.

Chintz Appliqué

Cut a single motif from a print fabric and appliqué it to your bag. Begin by rough-cutting the motif from your print fabric, leaving an inch or so outside the picture. Iron this piece onto fusible interfacing or iron-on adhesive. Trim the picture down, leaving an even amount of background outside the actual motif. This is easier to do accurately after the fabric has been stiffened by the interfacing or bonding paper. The purpose of leaving a border around the motif is so your stitches won't ruin the look of the motif.

Next pin the motif in place on the front of the tote bag. If you are using iron-on adhesive, peel off the backing and press the motif in place. Zigzag-stitch around the motif. Choose your thread to blend with the bag fabric or contrast sharply with the appliqué. Your stitches don't need to be exceedingly close together, especially if you've used the adhesive. In fact, you might get away with using the hemstitch on your machine. This looks very similar to a hand buttonhole stitch that is sometimes used for hand appliqué.

Original Appliqué

You can make your own appliqué out of fabric scraps. Draw your own picture, thinking in terms of different fabrics for each area. Decide which pieces can extend under other pieces so you only need one row of stitches to hold both pieces down. Draw these areas as dotted lines into the adjoining area.

Mark each individual piece with a number or letter. Make two or three copies of your picture and cut out the pieces so that you have a pattern for each fabric piece. You will need more than one copy for this because the dotted areas will need to be cut as part of two different pieces. Be sure to keep the original picture so you can put the puzzle back together.

Use the original drawing to trace the design onto the textured side of a piece of fusible interfacing or the adhesive side of iron-on adhesive. Put the appliqué together on top of this drawing like a puzzle. Press the pieces in place. Sew the pieces together and to the tote bag front as described above.

Embroidery

Either machine- or hand-embroider a picture or your name or even a motto onto your tote bag. This can relate to your intended use of the bag or your own personal convictions. "Follow Your Bliss" would be one of my Zen-inspired choices.

Counted Cross-Stitch

There are bags made out of cross-stitch fabric, but if you can't find one, or want to make your own bag, you can use waste fabric as a guide to cross-stitch the front of your bag. Waste fabric looks a little like very stiff cross-stitch fabric. Baste it onto your tote bag. Cross-stitch your design over the waste fabric and through your tote bag fabric, being careful not to split the threads of the waste fabric and removing the basting stitches as you come to them. When you are finished stitching, remove any remaining basting stitches and wet the fabric. The glue that holds the threads together will dissolve, allowing you to pull the threads of the waste fabric out from under your cross-stitches.

Other Ideas

You don't need to be limited to the conventional. Decorate your bag with scraps of ribbon, lace, or binding. Buttons will add dimension, as will sequins, charms, or beads. Use fabric paint or permanent markers or a combination of these ideas. Decorate the back, too, if you want.

Putting It All Together

Measuring from the center of the top, decide on the placement of the handles. With the right side of the tote bag facing you, lay out one handle in a "U" shape against the bag front. The raw edges of the handle pieces should extend at least 2" beyond the upper edge of the bag. These ends will be stitched to the facing later so there will be no danger of them pulling loose. Adjust this if you don't want your handles to be so long. If the seam on the handles is along one edge, place that edge toward the center of the "U" shape. If the seam is centered on one side, pin the handles so that the seam side is facing you, away from the bag. Sew the handles in place about ½" from the top edge of the bag. Repeat with the back of the bag, making sure your handles will line up across from each other and will be the same length.

Place the two facing pieces on top of the handles, right side down, lining up one edge with the top of the bag. Stitch ½" from this edge. Press the facing pieces up so they extend beyond the top of the bag over the raw edges of the handles. Trim the handle ends so that they are approximately ½" shorter than the facing. Sew them to the facing along the side edges and across the cut edge.

Fold the bag in half, right sides together, lining up the facing seams. Sew ½" from the edges along the sides of the bag and the facing. Zigzag stitch along this seam allowance to prevent it from fraying. Press the seam allowances toward the back of the bag.

Turn the raw edges of the facing pieces under ½" and stitch them down. This hem should cover the raw edges of the handles. Press the facing to the inside of the bag, folding along the seam with the body of the bag. Stitch the facing to the bag close to the hemmed edge through the bag if this top stitching won't interfere with your decoration. Hem it by hand if you need to.

Enjoy

Now that you've finished your bag, have you thought of more than one use for it? Do you wish you had done some things differently? Do you wish you had made it bigger or smaller? Brighter or dressier? Put this one to use and take another crack at it.

Zen Wall Hanging

Try your hand at making something purely for the fun of doing it. A wall hanging is a good choice because it reminds us of that most conventional art form: a painting. Your medium will be fabric primarily and anything else you want to stitch or glue to your work of art.

Lining and Backing

You will need to have a lining piece of some kind to sew the pieces of your creation onto. You may want to back it with another piece as well when you're done. Spend some time considering what fabrics will support your wall hanging yet will not be too difficult to sew with. Be sure you make your hanging large enough that you give yourself a good chance to be creative.

Since you will probably not be washing your wall hanging, you might want to refrain from washing your backing and lining fabrics before you begin. This will allow them to retain any sizing or finishes that make them just a little crisper and stiffer—something that might prove helpful with this project.

Design

You may want to spend some time with a pencil and paper sketching your design. If you are more comfortable with representational art than something more abstract, go ahead and plan in greater detail. Otherwise, just sketch a little to get your imagination started. For a project like this, think of your sketch more as a guide than a pattern. Plan to deviate from it as inspiration leads you in other directions.

Materials

Collect your materials together. Choose as wide a variety of textures as possible. Check the remnant binds in fabric stores. Consider fleece, fake fur, upholstery fabric, velvets, satins, and anything else you come across.

Don't confine your search to fabric. Consider ribbons, yarn, seam binding, twill tape, lace, and cords. How about adding beads, sequins, charms, buttons, or other fasteners?

Construction

Your construction techniques are going to depend on the materials you've chosen. You can use fabric glue, but I'd recommend you stitch as much as possible. Let the stitching be part of the whole picture, not just a means to an end. In fact, stitch with yarn and a tapestry needle if you want.

Remember, you probably won't be washing your wall hanging. Fraying is not as strong a concern here as it would normally be. In fact, fraying may be the look you are going for, since you are working in three dimensions instead of two. On the other hand, a clean edge might add to the look you're after. You may even prefer to turn some or all of the raw edges under.

Binding

Covering the outside edge of your hanging with some binding is not necessary, but may give it the finished look it needs. Think of the binding as the frame for your "painting." You can buy double-fold bias binding for this purpose or make your own. Consider what kind of frame will enhance your creation. A neutral color or something to match a color in the hanging might give it a formal look. A binding made from strips of several different fabrics might fit better with your design.

Hanging

Don't forget to add something to your wall hanging to make it possible to actually hang it. A sleeve across the back a few inches shorter than the width of the hanging is one idea. If the rod or dowel you run through the sleeve is shorter than the width of the hanging, it can balance on two nails and remain completely hidden.

Another suggestion is to add tabs that extend above the wall hanging. These are especially effective if you are hanging your creation from a decorative curtain rod.

Cleaning

Unless you've been careful about your fabric choices, you probably won't be able to wash your wall hanging. You can spot-wash any specks left by insects, but you'll need some method of cleaning the dust away. The deeper the dimensions on your hanging, the more dust it'll catch.

If your hanging is stitched securely, you could take it outside and shake the dust away. Be certain that it will hold up to this kind of pressure before you try it. A gentler, though also somewhat risky, method is to vacuum away the dust. Secure a thin cloth or netting over the nozzle of your vacuum cleaner. This will prevent any loose pieces from being torn off and sucked up by the vacuum. Carefully, lightly vacuum the surfaces where dust collects. Or you can blow dirt away with canned air used for cleaning computers.

You won't need to be afraid to hang your creation up where you can enjoy it.

Index